Does the Past Have a Future?:
The Political Economy of Heritage

Edited by Professor Sir Alan Peacock

Professor Sir Alan Peacock
Professor Bruno S. Frey
Professor Felix Oberholzer-Gee
Professor Ilde Rizzo
Professor Francoise Benhamou
David Sawers
Sir Gerald Elliot
Professor Dick Netzer

Published by The Institute of Economic Affairs
1998

First published in May 1998 by
The Institute of Economic Affairs
2 Lord North Street
Westminster
London SW1P 3LB

IEA Readings 47
All rights reserved
ISSN 0305-814X
ISBN 0-255 36414-8

Many IEA publications are translated into languages other than
English or are reprinted. Permission to translate or to reprint should
be sought from the General Director at the address above.

Printed in Great Britain by
Redwood Books, Trowbridge, Wiltshire
Set in Times Roman 11 on 12 point

Contents

FOREWORD

Colin Robinson

THE PAST IS IMPORTANT. The store of buildings, artefacts, books and cultural objects from the past embodies human experience and constitutes the source of our ability to learn. Indeed, since the future is unknowable and the present is ephemeral, in a real sense the past is all we have. Yet not all of it can be preserved. How can decisions best be made about what to preserve and who should make them? What constitutes our 'heritage' and how can we recognise what should be kept?

Such issues may seem remote from the normal work of the economist but, as **Sir Alan Peacock** explains in his Introduction to Readings 47, they have a significant economic aspect. Sir Alan – a distinguished Honorary Fellow of the Institute and an economist who pioneered research into 'unorthodox' areas such as the economics of education and the arts – points out that heritage activities involve decisions about the use of resources. Presenting the past '...as a source of satisfaction and inspiration to both present and future generations' carries a cost since the resources so used could have been employed in other ways.

In this substantial contribution to the literature on heritage policy, eight authors (including Sir Alan) explain the policies of different countries and make suggestions for reform. **Professor Ilde Rizzo**, of the University of Catania, discusses the case for regulation to control the 'stock of heritage' (buildings and works of art), drawing examples from Italy. **Professor Françoise Benhamou**, of Paris X University, describes and analyses how heritage policy has evolved in France. **Professor Dick Netzer**, of New York University, deals with international aspects of heritage policy – where consumers travel considerable distances to enjoy heritage services. **Professors Bruno Frey** and **Felix Oberholzer-Gee** consider the place for cost-benefit analysis in heritage preservation and recommend that citizens be given the right to vote on major preservation projects.

Sir Gerald Elliot looks critically at the unwillingness of museum directors and trustees to recognise and tackle economic issues: he sees entry charges not just as means of raising money but as a way of changing the attitudes of museums to their visitors. **David Sawers** examines the National Trust, which is the biggest British charity and largest English private landowner, concluding that it is '...the most successful British institution in the heritage field', able to teach lessons to other institutions seeking private funds.

Sir Alan sees merit in the National Trust model, provided subscribers are given more power. He also wants contributors to the National Lottery – a big source of funds for heritage projects – to be polled so their preferences can be taken into account. Moreover, he suggests that central and local government heritage services could be privatised, with museums and galleries run as non-profit institutions and vouchers or grants provided for particular groups. At the same time, owners of historic buildings would be given more freedom than now to adapt and extend them. There would be an 'intense cultural shock' for those in the heritage business but, Sir Alan says, the '...true test of the success of professional efforts to expand and improve appreciation of our heritage is the public's willingness to pay from its own pocket'.

As in all Institute publications, the views expressed in Readings 47 are those of the authors, not of the IEA (which has no corporate view), its Trustees, Advisers or Directors. Nevertheless, it commends the authors' clear analyses and imaginative proposals for reform as important contributions to public debate on heritage preservation.

May 1998

COLIN ROBINSON
Editorial Director, Institute of Economic Affairs, and Professor of Economics, University of Surrey

THE AUTHORS

Françoise Benhamou teaches Economics at Paris X University and at the Institut d'Études Politiques of Paris and Lille. She is a researcher at the Laboratoire d'Economie Sociale, Paris I University. She was an adviser to the French Minister of Culture for two years (1989-90) and in charge of the National Library for the Arts in Paris (1991-92). She is the author of *L'économie de la culture* (La Découverte, 1996), and various papers and administrative reports about heritage conservation, libraries management, cultural organisations, and cultural industries.

Sir Gerald Elliot spent his working life in industry, retiring from the chairmanship of Christian Salvesen PLC in 1988. He has had a number of public activities in cultural and economic fields, including chairman of the Scottish Arts Council and Scottish Opera, and a trustee of the National Museums of Scotland. He is a director of the recently built Edinburgh Festival Theatre and a trustee of the David Hume Institute, which he co-founded with Sir Alan Peacock in 1985.

Bruno S. Frey was born in Basel and is a Swiss citizen. He was Professor of Economics at the University of Constance (1970-77) and since then has held a chair in economics at the University of Zurich. He was Visiting Fellow at All Souls College, Oxford University, and the Institute for Advanced Studies in Berlin, Visiting Professor at the University of Chicago, as well as at several other universities. Among his recent publications are *International Political Economics, Democratic Economic Policy, Muses and Markets: Explorations in the Economics of the Arts, Economics as a Science of Behaviour*, and more recently *Not Just for the Money: An Economic Theory of Personal Motivation*. Several of these books have been translated into nine different languages, among them Japanese and Chinese.

Dick Netzer is Professor of Economics and Public Administration at the Robert F. Wagner Graduate School of Public Service, New

York University, where he has been for more than 35 years. His research has focussed on public finance, urban economics and, in recent years, the economics of the arts and culture. He has had numerous assignments as a member of official boards and commissions in the U.S., especially at the level of state and local governments, including that as a director for the past 22 years of the agency that oversees the finances of the City of New York. He is a past president of the Association for Cultural Economics International and is president of an American foundation that makes grants to needy painters, sculptors and printmakers.

Felix Oberholzer-Gee was born in Zug, Switzerland. He received his doctoral degree in economics from the University of Zurich. He is currently Assistant Professor at the Wharton School, University of Pennsylvania, where he teaches political economy and cost-benefit analysis.

Sir Alan Peacock, now 75, retired from his last full-time academic appointment as Vice Chancellor and Professor of Economics at the University of Buckingham in 1985, co-founded the David Hume Institute in that year and was its first Executive Director (1985-91). He is still 'enjoyably busy' writing on the political economy of public policy, covering such diverse fields as public choice analysis, the economics of the welfare state, the economics of civil justice and, unusually, the economics of the arts. He is a Fellow of the British Academy, the Royal Society of Edinburgh and the Italian National Academy and his longstanding connection with the IEA is recognised by an Honorary Fellowship. His latest publications include *Public Choice Analysis in Historical Perspective* (Cambridge, 1992) and *The Political Economy of Economic Freedom* (Edward Elgar, 1997).

Ilde Rizzo is Professor of Public Economics at the University of Catania. Her research interests include cultural economics, procurement, local public finance and the theory of collective decision-making. She edited *Cultural Economics and Cultural Policies*, jointly with Alan Peacock, and *Economic Perspectives on Cultural Heritage*, jointly with Michael Hutter. She is the author of *The Hidden Debt.*

David Sawers is a writer and consultant who specialises in applied economics. He spent 18 years as an economist in the government service, and has also worked as a journalist and an academic. His major publications are (with John Jewkes and Richard Stillerman) *The Sources of Invention* (1958), a classic study of industrial innovation and (with Ronald Miller) *The Technical Development of Modern Aviation* (1968) a study of innovation in the aircraft industry. For the IEA he has written, with Wilfred Altman and Dennis Thomas, *TV – From Monopoly to Competition – and Back?* (Hobart Paper 15, Revised Edition 1962*), Competition in the Air* (Research Monograph 41, 1987), *Should the Taxpayer Support the Arts?* (Current Controversies No. 10, 1993), and 'The Future of Public Service Broadcasting', in M.E. Beesley (ed.) *Markets and the Media* (Readings 43, 1996).

Acknowledgements

All editors are dependent on others in bringing together collections of papers. In this case my special thanks go to Christine Blundell and Michael Solly for their hard work and dedication in editing and typesetting this volume of Readings.

May 1998   A.T.P.

1

THE ECONOMIST AND HERITAGE POLICY:

A REVIEW OF THE ISSUES

Sir Alan Peacock

David Hume Institute, Edinburgh

1. Introduction

SHORTLY AFTER ASSUMING OFFICE AS SECRETARY OF
STATE FOR NATIONAL HERITAGE, Mr Chris Smith announced
that his title would be changed to reflect the more forward looking
attitude of the Labour Government. As he put it in a *Times* article
(15 July 1997) : 'Heritage looks to the past. We look to the future.'
The DNH has now become the Department of Culture, Media and
Sport (DCMS). Heritage may now be only a sub-set of Culture but
clearly there is a future for the past, if only because of the growing
demand by private citizens for services which inculcate appreciation
of our heritage and which is expressed in willingness to pay for such
services not only as taxpayers but also directly through entry
charges to historic buildings and the like, subscriptions to the
various suppliers of such services and through the extensive
purchase of books and mementoes of kinds which provide a
permanent record of visits.

Thus heritage may represent the past, but it provides important
present satisfactions to a wide range of citizens in different age and
income groups, occupations and regions. While it would be foolish
to dismiss arguments for concentrating more attention on cultural
activities reflecting contemporary life and understandable if a new
government adds a populist twist to these arguments, the fact
remains that the introduction to the world of the arts, particularly of
the young, is most frequently made through the local museum or
gallery. No Minister who has to take account of public taste can
afford to ignore this.

The general purpose of this paper is to explain how heritage

1

services are organised in the UK and how far they are delivered in a form which promotes the interests of those who are meant to benefit from them. This entails the presentation of how these services are operated (Section 2), how they are influenced by the supply of funding from both the public and private sectors and by regulatory measures (Section 3), and a critique of current policies (Section 4). Finally, some suggestions for reform are offered (Section 5) which are inevitably of a controversial character.

My approach has been markedly influenced by professional interest in heritage policies displayed by fellow economists, and particularly by the methods used by the authors of the essays which follow this one. It will soon be clear to the reader that these essays are not to be regarded solely as providing supplementary analysis and argument, but offer distinct contributions on important aspects of the debate on heritage policies. In particular, they indicate the growing importance not only of the interaction of ideas between professional economists that deserve presentation to a wider public, but also the extent to which heritage policies of different countries are becoming interdependent.

2. Heritage as an Economic Activity

Before considering the economic characteristics of heritage 'production', the reader should be warned that there is still widespread resistance to the very idea that anything to do with cultural pursuits of a 'high' order should be subjected to economic analysis. This resistance goes back to the bitter attack of Ruskin and his followers against the Classical Political Economists on the grounds that they were only concerned with material welfare. Of course, economists do tend to emphasise such objectives as a 'satisfactory' rate of economic growth, if only because the expansion of the material base improves the opportunities for using more resources to support cultural pursuits, but this is not the point at issue. Economics is concerned with the allocation of resources, however these are to be used, and the implications for individuals in society of their allocation in one way rather than another. As heritage activities involve decisions about the use of resources, in this sense there is an economic aspect. Nowadays, one suspects that while this argument is fully understood by museum directors and those managing heritage sites because they are faced with difficult allocative decisions of their own, they continue to press the case for special immunity from economic analysis.[1] I shall argue later that this hardly helps their case.

In identifying heritage services, a distinction is usually made between the 'built heritage' and the presentation of moveable historical artefacts in 'museums and galleries'. This emphasises the heterogeneous nature of the services but, broadly speaking, the various forms of their delivery represent specific sectors of culture in which the services are substitutes for one another. While the general characteristic of such services is a fixed location, one must take account of the growing influence of technology on the final output, now that video tapes offer guided tours of historic homes and locations without actually visiting them, and offer even custom-built viewing of pictures in famous galleries. The parallel here with tapes and CDs of music and drama indicates a strong element of complementarity between the modes of delivery.

Heritage Production

There are some special features of heritage production that have a bearing on heritage policy:

- A large proportion of artefacts was not originally produced with the idea of reminding future generations of their heritage, but as means for satisfying contemporary tastes, typically of rich aristocrats and of the Church, though there are exceptions such as war memorials. Artefacts become identified as heritage goods usually by receiving the *imprimatur* of archaeologists and historians, officially recognised as those most competent to determine their historical significance. Their influence is consolidated by their employment in senior positions in the heritage services, particularly in the public sector. However, whereas the public sector plays a major rôle in heritage provision, the developing interest in the past has recently stimulated private entry into the heritage business on a considerable scale. Professional reaction has been rather like that of the BBC towards commercial TV in the 1950s with strong attacks on 'fringe' heritage organisations which promote

---

[1] Peter Cannon-Brookes, 'Cultural-Economic Analysis of Art Museums: a British Curator's Point of View', in V.A. Ginsburgh and P. M. Menger (eds.), *Economics of the Arts*, Amsterdam: Elsevier, 1996.

inventions in the past which cater for crude antiquarianism or Disney-like fantasies.[2]

- The stock of 'professionally recognised' heritage artefacts represents a process of accretion rather than a form of organised production. Its potential stock cannot respond to collective or individual demands for possession other than by a process of discovery or by the passage of time which transfers once-new creations into a legacy of past treasures. Growing public and private demand for access to or possession of historical artefacts has stimulated the process of discovery. Apart from illicit practices within the private art market, governments have accelerated the process of accretion by various measures designed to induce and even force private owners of artefacts to reveal their existence, to preserve those identified as part of the national heritage, and to oblige private owners to display them to the public. Regulation has therefore played a major part in the attempt to adjust supply to demand.[3]

- The stock of artefacts, combined with the knowledge of its significance which viewers get from visits to sites, lectures, books, TV and videos, provides direct satisfaction, but a large part of the stock is acquired by museums and galleries in particular and is not displayed or seen by members of the public. It is claimed by Pommerehne and Frey[4] that the display/stock ratio is rarely more than 1 to 4 with the Prado representing the extreme case where less than 10 per cent of the stock of objects has been on display. The usual justification for this situation is that, apart from limitations of display space, museums and galleries also provide services to researchers. The implication is that the public must benefit in some way or other as the providers of revenue and charges for such activities, giving rise to the question as to the nature of these benefits and their magnitude.

---

[2] See the well-known attack by Robert Hewison, *The Heritage Industry : Britain in a Climate of Decline*, London: Methuen, 1987.

[3] These matters are analysed further in the papers by Drs Benhamou and Rizzo in this volume.

[4] The *locus classicus* for the detailed examination of museum behaviour is Bruno Frey and Werner Pommerehne, *Muses and Markets*, Oxford: Basil Blackwell, 1989.

- The peculiarities observed in the accretion and utilisation of the capital input to heritage services are matched by the characteristics of labour supply. The estimates of the size and growth in labour input vary widely, depending on the quality of data about the private sector, knowledge of whose activities seems to depend on what contact it has with government funding sources and with the regulatory system. The exceptions are the main private 'suppliers' of heritage services, namely the National Trusts of England and Wales and of Scotland. Estimates of those engaged in built heritage and museums and galleries employment vary but in the mid-1990s, estimates suggest about 90,000 persons. The striking fact is that about 26,000 were volunteers, 53 per cent of whom worked at heritage sites and 47 per cent in museums and galleries. A separate estimate for the National Trust of England and Wales cites a figure of 28,000 volunteers working for them, but this figure includes those engaged on nature conservation. Nearly a quarter of private sector museums appeared to rely entirely on voluntary labour.[5]

- As in many other countries, the official suppliers of heritage services, and also a large proportion of independent suppliers, operate on a non-profit basis. One need not get into an argument about whether some profit target, including minimising losses, could be used as an indicator of efficient running of such suppliers, for the fact is that such an idea is far removed from reality. In contrast with the recent past – in which it was sufficient for famous heritage providers, notably our national museums, to produce annual reports written in impeccable English, finely printed and often containing beautiful illustrations but with magisterial statements on their 'progress' despite the niggardly nature of their public grants – nowadays, 'corporate plans' are rightly insisted upon by the public heritage authorities. This requires the identification of performance indicators and the comparison of performance targets with out-turn.

---

[5] For this and further information on employment, see Bernard Casey, Rachael Dunlop and Sara Selwood, *Culture as Commodity*, London: Policy Studies Institute, 1995, Ch. 3.

Peer Group Assessment and 'Excellence'

Heritage managers have a clear interest in the choice of such indicators and seem to have no trouble in convincing government-sponsoring departments that they should be based on 'peer group assessment'. As put by the influential Museums and Galleries Commission (1992):[6]

> '[A]ll museums should state and monitor in their corporate plans and annual reports the intellectual standards at which they are aiming... larger museums should introduce peer group review to help in the mutual assessment of this aspect of their work.'

There is nothing exceptional in this arrangement, which is widely accepted by public bodies concerned with higher education and research and cultural matters generally. Whether performance indicators devised by the peer group are closely correlated with the interests of those providing the funding is another matter.

Consider the following Table derived from the Annual Report and Accounts (1996-1997) and Corporate Plan (1997-2000) for Historic Scotland:[7]

Table 1: Selected Key Performance Targets (1996-97) Set by the Secretary of State for Scotland

A. Protecting Scotland's Built Heritage	*Target*	*Achieved*
1) Number of monuments scheduled	370	373
2) Number of historic building repair projects	145	145
B. Promoting and Presenting the Built Heritage		
1) Share of visitors to historic properties	47%	50%
2) Proportion of satisfied visitors (based on surveys)	95%	97%
3) Average spend per visitor	£1.02	£1.09

---

[6] See their report, *Museums Matter*, London, 1992, p.50.

[7] Historic Scotland, *Annual Reports and Accounts 1996-1997 and Corporate Plan 1997-2000*, Edinburgh: The Stationery Office, 23 July 1997. This document is an outstanding example of 'best practice'.

The division of indicators into protection and promotion of heritage artefacts makes sense, the former representing the interests of 'future generations' and the latter those of present generations as visitors to historic sites. The principal target for protection is really an input rather than an output measure and the individual items in it can hardly be homogeneous, but one may concede that new additions to the capital stock could be a necessary but hardly a sufficient condition for guaranteeing benefits in the future. The use of visitor share and visitor satisfaction indicators might give a general idea of benefits conferred on present generations. But there is no information concerning the fixing of the targets themselves and their perceived relative importance. These matters are presumably a matter of negotiation between the sponsoring department of the Scottish Office and Historic Scotland.

However, the extent of the progress made by Historic Scotland in recognising responsibility for justifying its activities may be gauged by considering the very different attitude of the British Museum which holds a singularly important position in museum culture, not only in Britain but internationally. The recent fundamental review of the British Museum's operations[8] drew attention to the professional *ethos* of its management in some striking paragraphs from which the following excerpts are taken:

- 'The Museum has a well-established "sotto voce" approach to external affairs. The magnificent collections are deemed to speak for themselves' (para. 2.4.2).

- '[T]he Museum has not seen itself as needing to attract audiences in a competitive market and has not thought it necessary to take special steps to stimulate public excitement or enthusiasm' (para. 2.4.3).

- '[P]ublic relations are reactive rather than pro-active. No special effort is made to inform the public what the Museum has to offer' ... 'If the Museum wishes to acquire important objects, it prefers that no one should know' (para. 2.4.4).

---

[8] The British Museum, *A Fundamental Review of the Museum's Operations*, prepared by Andrew Edwards, 8 October 1996.

- 'The image of excellence is seen as all-important. Vulgarity is to be avoided at all costs' ... *'The approval of scholars and scholarly journalists is seen as the dominating objective and its achievement as the highest accolade the Museum can receive'* (my italics) (para. 2.4.5).

- 'Its general preference is to minimise dealings with external constituencies.... There is no policy to promote open, friendly, constructive, co-operative or warm relationships' (para. 2.4.6).

It is noteworthy that the British Museum, although now under pressure fully to justify its position, had until 1996 produced neither a regular annual report nor found it necessary to prepare and publish a recognisable corporate plan.

3. Heritage Funding

As already indicated, both the private and public sectors provide heritage services, but that is not to say that the former is financed entirely from private sources and the latter from public sources. An additional complication is that it is not always easy to determine to which sector a particular heritage service belongs. A suitable way of sorting out the relative importance of the different parts of heritage provision is to present the reader with a Flow of Funds system which identifies the suppliers, allocators, spenders and users of heritage finance.

A broad schema is set out in Figure 1 showing the passage of funds from their origin to their use. Without going into great detail, we can identify the 'actors', reading from left to right. Clearly, *Households* are the ultimate source of *all* finance, either in the form of taxation, donations, or payments for services rendered, though it simplifies the system by identifying *Firms* as a donor of funding. They are classified as the *SUPPLIERS* of funding. The *ALLOCATORS* are divided into *Government, Private Foundations and Households*. *Central Government* allocates funding mainly through the DCMS (formerly DNH) but, while it owns a large proportion of the historic properties, it turns over their management to a number of separate bodies, of which English Heritage is the most important *Quango*. A number of government departments, notably the Ministry of Defence, run their own museums. *Local Authorities* allocate funding mainly to museums and galleries, most

Figure 1: Heritage Funding: A Schematic Diagram of the Passage of Funds from Origins to Uses

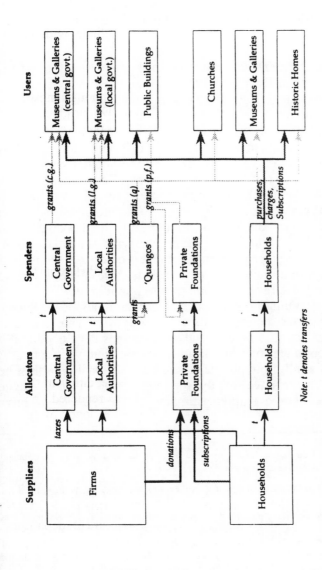

of which they own and operate. The most important of the *Private Foundations* is the National Trust which is an independent organisation with charitable status, whose activities as a 'permanent' preserver of lands and buildings of historic interest are recognised in Acts of Parliament.[9] It relies mainly, on private sources, subscriptions and donations, but these attract substantial tax relief.

Turning to *SPENDERS*, the noteworthy feature of the British system is the use of Boards of Trustees (with government-appointed members) to manage National Museums and Galleries in England and Wales and in Scotland, together with Executive Agencies, notably English Heritage and its Scots counterpart Historic Scotland, and the agencies managing the Royal Parks and Royal Palaces. We have classified them using the popular nomenclature of *Quangos* (Quasi Autonomous National Government Organisations) though in official parlance they are known as Non-Departmental Public Bodies. Finally, *USERS* are classified broadly according to their 'ownership' though this might give a false impression of their rights of disposal of property. The main point to note is that a large proportion of public sector users charge for admission or hire of their facilities, whereas correspondingly private sector users receive revenue funding from public sources.[10]

This brief account of the pattern of financial relations between the public and private sectors needs filling out with data, but it is a significant reflection on the way that policy has developed that the relative importance of the various financial flows cannot be calculated, if at all, from published sources. The main problem here is that the provenance of the private sector is only vaguely determinable. For example, estimates of the number of private

---

[9] The activities of the National Trust are critically examined in detail in the contribution of David Sawers to this volume (Chapter 5).

[10] For definitional detail, see Alan Peacock, 'A Future for the Past : The Political Economy of Heritage', British Academy Keynes Lecture 1994, in *Proceedings of the British Academy*, Oxford: Oxford University Press, 1996. Data have been extracted from various tables in *Cultural Trends No.26*, Policy Studies Institute, 1997, pp. 72 *et seq.* For the institutional and historical detail, see the excellent survey of Stephen Creigh-Tyte, 'The Development of British Policy on Built Heritage Preservation', in Michael Hutter and Ilde Rizzo (eds.), *Economic Perspectives on Cultural Heritage*, London: Macmillan, 1997, Ch. 8.

museums and galleries classifiable as heritage suppliers are understandably approximations, a figure of 1,500 being given by the Association of Independent Museums.

An attempt is made in Table 2 to trace the links between *Spenders* and *Users* in order to give some idea of the pattern of funding in 1993/94. The Table has huge gaps in it, because of lack of data. In particular, three require mention :

- Only a very small number of independent museums and galleries has been included, and only because data are confined to those which receive direct public funding;

- *Churches* have been omitted from the Table because of lack of data;

- The estimates for business and private foundation sources of finance are shaky – hence the brackets.

The National Trust is not shown as a Private Foundation but its income from private sources is listed under *Households*. However, even with these defects, it may be safely concluded that government, directly or through quangos such as English Heritage, exerts a major influence on heritage provision both through its ownership of heritage artefacts and the provision of funding to both public and private institutions.

Funding, however, is only one part of the story of control over heritage provision, as already indicated. The 'availability' of heritage capital inputs depends on an active policy to identify, conserve and manage them and this has led successive governments to strengthen official control over both public and private artefacts. The process begins with the compilation of a record of historic buildings and ancient monuments compiled by the Royal Commission on the Historical Monuments of England (RCHME) which employs a large staff of archaeologists and historians. Latterly, DNH and now DCMS has worked on a list of about 1,600 historical buildings in government ownership in order to monitor arrangements for repair and maintenance.

It is the scheduling system operated by DCMS with advice from English Heritage which identifies ancient monuments, archaeological remains, and the listing of buildings of architectural merit which places important restrictions on the use of private

Table 2: Sources and Uses of Heritage Funding : England, 1993-94 (in £million)

Sources	Central Government	Local Government	Quangos	Households	Private Foundations	Total	% of total
Grants	201	142	105	-	(37)	485	73
Charges }	-	-	-}		-		
Subscriptions}	-	-	-}	179	-	179	27
Sales }	-	-	-}		-		
Total Sources	**201**	**142**	**105**	**179**	**(37)**	**664**	**100**
Uses							
Museums Galleries (General Government)	189	-	-	73	(30)	292	44
Museums Galleries (Local Government)	-	???		??	-	110	17
English Heritage	-	32	105	15	(7)	159	24
Museums/Galleries (Private Sector)	12	?	-	8	-	20	3
Historic Homes (Private Sector)	-	-	-	83	-	83	12
Total Uses (£m)	**201**	**142**	**105**	**179**	**(37)**	**664**	**100**
% of total	**30**	**21**	**16**	**27**	**6**	**100**	

Source: Compiled by the author from sources listed in footnote 10, p. 10.

property by its owners. No fewer than 600,000 archaeological sites of 'national importance', mostly located in rural areas, are estimated as identifiable to be protected by legislation, and by the year 2003 it is estimated that 45,000 of them will be so protected. Even more important for private owners is the process of listing buildings, grading them according to their degree of historical and architectural importance, the term 'building' being interpreted widely to include walls, fountains, bridges and even telephone boxes. Something like half a million individual buildings are listed for England and Wales, but only about 6 per cent of them are considered to be of such importance that restrictions on alteration or demolition will be rigorously enforced.

Moveable artefacts are now covered by the Treasure Act of 1996 (which 'nationalises' all discoveries of gold and silver artefacts – discoveries that have proceeded apace with the development of the metal detector). Disputes are frequent about the amount and distribution of payment for these 'finds' as between discoverers and owners of the land on which they have been made, and national museums have tried to use their 'clout' to keep the best discoveries for themselves.[11] Finally, passing mention should be made of the restrictions on the export of moveable artefacts which may be applied on the recommendation of the Reviewing Committee on the Export of Works of Art. Exports of major works of art require a licence and this alerts the Committee to make recommendations as to whether such works are of 'national importance'. If so considered, the DCMS can defer granting of the licence in order to allow an offer of purchase to be made which would keep the work in the country.

The funding arrangements and regulation corroborate the previous observations about the power and influence over heritage matters exercised by professional cadres, both as advisers and managers of heritage services. They have considerable discretion in deciding on the extent to which they should take account of the interest of those who fund their activities, the public at large as taxpayers, patrons, subscribers or consumers. These professionals have increasingly been put in the position of justifying their claim that they do act in the public interest, particularly as a result of the

---

[11] For an interesting discussion of this issue, see Andrew Selkirk, *Who Owns the Past?*, London: Adam Smith Institute, 1997, Ch. 4.

long-term worries of government about keeping its expenditure under control. That claim is now examined in detail and leads naturally to consider what policy changes might be sensibly made.

4. The Political Economy of Heritage Provision

Most services are provided through the market economy, including heritage services by independent museums and galleries, owners of historical homes and monuments, on the assumption that consumers are competent to make their own decisions about the amount and composition of their purchases. In the long run, the interplay of the evolution of individuals' tastes and the change in their economic situation with innovations in the methods of presentation of historical 'experiences' will alter the dimensions of the market. Under conditions of uncertainty, suppliers may misjudge the public's demand for particular services and customers may regret their choices but, with competition in supply, the costs of acquiring consumer information and interpreting it may be made sufficiently small to enable consumers to reduce the incidence of disappointment. The dynamic process of the market will therefore do much to further the aim of maximising the satisfaction of consumers.

It is well established that there must be qualifications to this argument which apply over a wide range of markets for services, mainly associated with externalities of production and consumption and which certainly apply in the heritage field.[12] These will be briefly examined, but it must be clear from the account given of the provision of heritage services in the UK that the perceived range of qualifications is much wider, otherwise it would be difficult to explain how it has come about that heritage supply is dominated by non-market provision. A critical examination of these arguments offers the clue to suggestions for a reconsideration of official policies which have hardly altered for decades, whatever the hue of the government in power.

---

[12] A more extensive examination of the externality problems extended to consider the international demand for and supply of heritage is contained in Dick Netzer's contribution to this volume (Chapter 7).

'Public Goods' Arguments

Taking the traditional arguments first, we can certainly identify historical artefacts that have 'public goods' characteristics, in the economist's sense that they are 'indivisible' and 'non-excludable' so that market pricing becomes impossible or at least difficult and their provision depends either on voluntary action or compulsory levies. Indivisibility means that viewing enjoyment by one person does not preclude similar enjoyment by others, at least to the point of congestion. My viewing of the magnificent panorama of the Castle Rock at Edinburgh does not restrict the view of others. If we measure the 'output' of this vista as individual visits, production costs fall to zero as 'output' increases, making a case for free viewing in order to maximise consumer benefits. However, in this case, I can benefit from the vista whether I am prepared to pay or not, and if there is escape for one there is escape for all. The market solution assumes that non-payers can be excluded from enjoying the service, and so breaks down. Hence the argument at least for public *financing* of heritage services which are public goods that would otherwise deteriorate and even fall down.

How many artefacts fall into this category is an empirical question. There is a tendency for those who promote public action to exaggerate the extent of 'publicness', notably by muddying the meaning of the term 'public good' to mean 'public weal', which is an altogether different concept. It is certainly technically possible to prevent access to museums and galleries unless payment is made. Moreover, whatever the force of the argument for free access on the grounds of zero marginal costs, the question still remains as to who is going to pay the total costs of maintaining and preserving artefacts. The problem is further complicated by the fact that supply of the information required to enjoy the experience of viewing such 'public goods' can exclude non-payers, as in the case of 'on-the-spot' video presentation of the historical events associated with the artefact and the sale of video-tapes to savour the experience after the event.

A second argument used by the pundits to justify public intervention claims that consumer sovereignty is not in the interests of consumers themselves and does not take account of the interests of those who cannot express their choices through the market, notably future generations. The choice of the artefacts to be preserved and displayed or stored is best left to experts if the 'true' interests of the public are to be served. It will be readily conceded that private individuals recognise that there are 'externalities of consumption' which benefit them and which support this line of argument. Even those who discern no benefit for themselves from the supply of heritage services will recognise that they can derive satisfaction from the availability of this benefit to others. Rich donors may derive personal satisfaction from substantial gifts of artefacts because of a genuine desire to benefit the public, as well as from preserving the memory of themselves and their family. The less well-off may derive comparable satisfaction from supporting access to heritage services for their children as part of their educational and cultural development, and feel uncomfortable at the thought that future generations will be far from pleased if artefacts are destroyed which can never be re-created. This may rationally entail leaving experts to choose for them, although this certification process may be thought of rather as a contractual arrangement, carrying with it the right ultimately to reject vicarious choices, if not through direct payment for the services then by the ballot box.

However, the argument is used to support institutional arrangements which accord with a desire to 'ring fence' heritage production from any form of debate about its content originating from those outside the charmed circle of experts.[13] It is not as if experts always agree amongst themselves about what is worth preserving for future generations: the more thoughtful of them recognise that aesthetic judgments in the final analysis are subjective, albeit informed ones.[14] The possibility that the tremendous planned expansion in archaeological and historical sites and the extension of the listing of an ever-growing schedule of buildings may entail an opportunity cost must never be entertained. The optimal expansion appears almost to be illimitable in the interests of preserving the 'integrity' of our heritage as the past recedes. It is being mildly cynical, but I believe accurate, to observe that the opportunity cost problem must never be mentioned, because any recognition of a limitation on resources available for the identification, preservation and display of heritage artefacts will

---

[13] See the attack on the author in Cannon-Brookes, *op.cit.*

[14] See the important discussion by the doyen of art historians, Sir Ernst Gombrich, in his 'Art History and the Social Sciences', *Ideals and Idols : Essays on Values in History and in Art*, London: Phaidon Press, 1979.

draw attention to the disagreements amongst experts as to how limited resources should be used, making it a palpable breach of professional conduct.

The assumption that the development of heritage services is purely a matter for art and architectural historians, archaeologists and the like and that they should also manage these services is translatable into forceful opposition to the intrusion of sensible economic practices. One cannot better the excellent and witty account of this opposition by the Chicago economist William Grampp in his wide-ranging survey of museum and gallery (MG) practices in Europe and America.[15] As he demonstrates:

- *acquisitions* by non-commercial MG managers are rarely justified, even in general terms, by reference to an evaluation of the benefits to be derived from them by those providing the purchase cost – visitors (if charged), benefactors and taxpayers;

- *capital value* of heritage assets is not to be calculated because the value of art cannot be expressed in terms of money because of its 'intrinsic worth'.

Aside from the obvious economic nonsense of not admitting that heritage capital is scarce and must have a price reflecting that scarcity, this is a highly convenient position. If accepted, it means that no account need be given of the efficient use of capital, which could be compared with use of government funds for alternative cultural activities, it militates against strict inventory control, and it removes the necessity for revealing criteria for the storing and preservation of artefacts. Anecdotes abound on the extraordinary laxity of inventory control by museums and galleries. For example, the Art Institute of Chicago lost a painting by a prominent American artist which had to be declared 'missing' but only after 10 years from the discovery. 'It could have been taken out with the garbage,' remarked the then director. The same Institute stored Impressionist works in a broom cupboard, lost them, but fortunately they were recovered. The classic case is the V&A which did not know that a Tenier was missing until it was found by the police and returned!

---

[15] William Grampp, 'A Colloquy about Arts Museums: Economics Engages Museology', in Ginsburgh and Menger, *op.cit.*, Ch. 9.

Admission Charges

Although by far from being exclusive to the UK (as Grampp makes clear), two particular suggestions about MG practice exercise their managers and have led to a long-lasting campaign to lobby their government paymasters with the support of their professional confrères. The first is *admission charges*. 'Most people working in UK museums would instinctively prefer to see no charge for admission' (Museums and Galleries Commission, 1992). Our line of argument suggests that this position is derived from rational behaviour and not from 'instinct'. If charging were to become a major source of revenue, then professional habits would have to change radically. Revenue would have to be earned through attraction of custom, in competition (perish the thought!) against both other state and independent museums already practised in the art of marketing, and could require adapting display to popular demand thus interfering with 'their proper work which is to exhibit, conserve and study the art that in the opinion of museum professionals is most deserving of attention'.[16]

Support for non-charging can easily be mustered from art critics with a comparative advantage in rhetorical flourish. Thus Brian Sewell, art critic of *The Evening Standard*:

> 'The museum habit – enquiry, information, wonderment – is a custom to be stimulated in every living soul in this country, easy, casual, familiar; but the hefty admission charge is a serious deterrent that makes visiting a museum and entertainment as luxurious and élite as Covent Garden opera, and not the commonplace of daily life.'[17]

The costs falling on staff, who would have to undergo training in marketing charm or be joined by rank outsiders already equipped with such skills, would extend to the possibility that hours of opening might have to conform with the convenience of visitors. Something more than a blanket admission charge would be necessary to attract custom, requiring even differential pricing by time of day, for concessionaires, and even including the purchase of

---

[16] Grampp, *ibid.*, quoting *Art in America*, June 1986.

[17] Brian Sewell, 'Admission Charges: An Argument Against', *The Art Quarterly*, National Art Collections Fund, No. 30, Summer 1997.

tickets through commercial agencies. The whole *ethos* of the professional approach to heritage provision thus comes under threat.

'De-Accessioning'

The second issue concerns *de-accessioning*.[18] This awkward term simply means *selling* (or exchanging) artefacts, a practice to which museologists raise profound objections. The rationale for opposition rests on a series of arguments, aesthetic, even philosophical, and practical. One common to several countries is that no artefacts should be disposed of, even if they are not currently well-regarded by specialists, quite apart from the tastes and preferences of viewers, because aesthetic views change and future generations may be 'cheated' if a particular period or school is not represented. This is a clear admission of the fallibility of expert judgement, which encourages a risk-averse position rather like that of those who spread financial risks by holding a whole range of different types of securities and who only alter their portfolio through accumulation.

A more interesting view expressed forcibly by Cannon-Brookes (*op.cit.*) is that the traditional rôle of museums and galleries should be 'object-based'. Objects are accumulated for their information value and are conserved and researched by MGs themselves or by accredited scholars so that 'for the object-based museum its collections are its *raison d'être* and its intellectual history is embodied in them to the extent that de-accessioning is liable to compromise its integrity and falsify the record'. One can sympathise with the view that dispassionate scholarship and lack of commitment to a particular 'theme' is a protection against attempts by governments to use museums and galleries for propaganda purposes, but it is tantamount to arguing that MG managers should be given a blank cheque and can ignore the public who supply them with resources. Nor is it immediately obvious than an object-based policy precludes altering the amount and composition of artefacts but rather the opposite. There is surely a case for at least marginal changes in the stock as a way of achieving balanced collections which accord with the tenets of an object-based approach.

The further rationalisation of no de-accessioning is the allegedly practical reason that collections in public museums as state property

---

[18] A subject covered *in extenso* in Sir Gerald Elliot's paper in this volume (Chapter 6).

are inalienable. Moreover, state collections will include gifts from private donors who have given them, often on the clear understanding that they will not be disposed of. Selling such gifts would be a breach of trust and would discourage future donations. To place the onus on the government for the prevention of altering the mix of assets in order to improve heritage services is a convenient rationalisation. It is more likely to be a reflection of 'aesthetic capture' by the cultural establishment who find it convenient to claim that their hands are tied. One also wonders whether donors who demand that the offer of gifts depends on non-disposal at any time in the future have solely the interests at heart of those they wish to benefit, and not also the utility they derive from the preservation of their memory and any tax advantages in bequeathing artefacts to the nation.

Professional support for accumulation of historical artefacts as an end in itself extends, *mutatis mutandis*, to the built heritage. The parallel here with the more extreme versions of environmentalism is irresistible. Just as all living creatures are accorded rights of existence, including presumably fleas on dogs, evidently so, too, do historic buildings have an inalienable right to survival and preservation.[19] One is invited to believe not only that ourselves, our children and our children's children will be 'cheated' if a large part of physical evidence of the past is not preserved, but also that our souls will be in danger.

5. Agenda for a Heritage Policy

The purpose of a heritage policy should be to present the past as a source of satisfaction and inspiration to both present and future generations, bearing in mind that resources used for this purpose have alternative uses which may be used to improve welfare in other ways. The public itself should be the arbiters in determining the size of the 'heritage sector' as manifested in the direct financial support it is willing to give to suppliers of heritage services, both private and public, and in the taxes and other compulsory levies it sanctions as voters/taxpayers in recognition of the need for public finance to cover desired heritage services that a market cannot supply. Of course, these are liberalist value-judgements though

---

[19] This position is defended in A. Brennan, 'Moral Pluralism and the Environment', *Environmental Values*, Vol. 1, No.1, 1992, pp.15-33.

surely widely accepted, but if they are accepted, then considerable changes are needed in the conduct of present heritage policy.

In recent times heritage policy has modified the patrician stance taken by the public authorities towards the public. Therefore it may seem that all that is necessary is to continue to strengthen the strands of protection offered by administrative devices so that public money is well spent. Briefly summarised, these are:

- The setting out of heritage expenditure plans in annual reports of the DNH (now DCMS) and equivalent authorities in Wales and Scotland within the framework of Public Expenditure Plans which are submitted for parliamentary approval in the familiar way.

- Accounting checks by the National Audit Commission and reported to Parliament, particularly to its Heritage Committee, which monitor administrative practices and comment on matters requiring explanation and justification.

- The growing insistence on the presentation of Corporate Plans, by both executive agencies such as English Heritage and Historic Scotland and national museums and galleries, which specify performance indicators and performance targets and how far such targets are being reached.

- Encouragement to competitive tendering in award of contracts, for example, for restoration work.

- Regular surveys of public attitudes to heritage services and publication of the results.

- Decisions which impinge directly on the public, nationally or regionally, may be taken only after a public inquiry or an open process of consultation.

- The composition of the numerous advisory bodies and of the boards of executive agencies should include persons who are considered capable of gauging the sensitivities of the public as well as those who have professional knowledge.

- Regulations designed to restrict private disposal of heritage artefacts (which, if anything, are more liberal than those in other countries).

These administrative arrangements have much to commend them, but they postulate the existence of a clear and consistent policy for heritage provision which has transparent public support. Policy aims at present are couched in vague terms such as 'safeguarding the nation's heritage'. While obfuscation allows politicians and administrators to offer whatever interpretation is convenient, it is an evasion of responsibility not to clarify the principles underlying such a policy, how practice could accord with them, and how to involve the public more directly in their discussion. The elements of such a policy that might have wide appeal and would not unduly shock those who would have to carry it out in both the private and the public sector are now presented.

Towards a Sustainable Level of Heritage Allocation

A basic principle is that the preservation of the past is not some segregated element in the list of benefits to humankind, but consists of inputs of resources which must be shown to contribute to our welfare in a more effective way than in any alternative use. 'Discoveries' of historical artefacts which depend on such uncertainties as artistic fashions, the state of the weather, and the incidence of private sales listed in dealers' catalogues cannot in themselves determine the pace of supply of heritage services. The idea that there is some moral commitment to preserve everything identified by *cognoscenti* is a Ruskinite fantasy. The most that one can concede to this view, now fortunately regarded by sensible archaeologists and others as extreme, is that we look for some 'sustainable' level of heritage which can stand up to comparison with alternative uses of capital resources as perceived and determined by society at large.[20]

The rôle of the experts should be directed towards offering advice on the general *composition* of historical artefacts which are

---

[20] The implications of this approach are explored in more detail in David Throsby, 'Culture, Economics and Sustainability', *Journal of Cultural Economics*, Vol. 19, No.3, 1995, pp.1-8, and in Alan Peacock, 'Towards a Workable Heritage Policy', in Michael Hutter and Ilde Rizzo (eds.), *Economic Perspectives on Cultural Heritage*, London: Macmillan, 1997.

representative of our cultural heritage. This approach recognises that there must be a resource constraint on those preservation responsibilities which may be assigned to government. It can incorporate a risk-averse position on preservation, necessary to anticipate changes not only in the evolution of expert opinion but also uncertainty about what future generations might regard as worth preserving, offering a minimum guarantee that good examples of 'irreplaceable' historical artefacts are there for future generations to appraise. A typology of heritage artefacts with reference to historical period, different art-forms and domestic cultures must be implicit in any government policy governed by resource constraints, but there are two differences with existing practice which are necessary to establish the credibility of expert opinion. The first is that considerable changes would be necessary in the organisation of the supply of heritage services, as outlined below. The second is that the subjective if informed judgement of experts needs to be made sensitive to public opinion, particularly in the case where the 'publicness' of heritage services must entail financing them through taxation.

Frey and Oberholzer[21] argue forcibly for the use of referenda for this purpose. Referenda reduce the discretionary rôles of politicians and their bureaucratic and professional advisers and come closer to registering individual preferences than contingent valuation studies. Such referenda should enable citizens to claim the right to vote on the size of the heritage budget, to approve or reject large heritage projects, and to initiate plans for new projects. Governments would still formulate heritage policies and control the budgetary process which gives them effect, but the right of challenge would be there if sufficient citizens decided to exercise it. They claim that the very existence of that right will alert politicians and officials to public concerns, including the distributional effects.

This is an attractive set of proposals but I have to rule it out for practical considerations, so far as Britain is concerned. The first problem is that it is difficult to single out the arts component of government budgets for special treatment, and extending the principle to the entire government budget would entail intolerable delay in the decision-making process. The second is that response to voter/taxpayer pressures through referenda is only likely to be

---

[21] In their contribution to this volume, see below, Chapter 2, pp. 44-52.

successful where close contact exists between government and citizens, as in confederations of the Swiss type and as part of a general tradition of continuing scrutiny of government measures. Much though one might prefer such a system of government, working within the constraint of a highly centralised system such as our own, albeit now to be modified by a measure of Celtic decentralisation, requires the search for an alternative.

Such an alternative may be found in direct public participation in the governance of such bodies as English National Heritage and Historic Scotland and insistence that publicly-funded (either by grants or by tax reliefs on covenanted income) heritage institutions, notably the National Trusts (see David Sawers, Chapter 5, below), should allow their subscribing members more power. This is not a simple endorsement of the present policy by which 'lay' persons without an obvious personal or professional axe to grind are nominated by the governing bodies of such institutions. Subscribers would themselves elect their own representatives. This is hardly a perfect solution for those most attracted to subscribe who may represent only the special interests of a minority, probably retired persons. However, it is compatible with other parts of the agenda for reform considered below. Additionally, those subscribing to the National Lottery, a major source of capital funding for heritage projects, should be polled and their preferences taken fully into account in deciding on the amount and composition of heritage provision.[22]

The idea of sustainable heritage coupled with the identification of representative historical artefacts, while necessary in order to give focus to proposals to conserve irreplaceable buildings and works of art that it is in no-one's individual interest to provide, should not be afforded some canonical status. If it were, it could be used to suppress competition between suppliers of heritage services and place unnecessary restrictions on the change of use and the adaptation of historic buildings and the sale of artefacts.

Privatisation and Public Preferences

The question that occurs to the economist is why cannot heritage services at present provided by central and local government be

---

[22] I have explored this matter further in 'Roll up for a National Lottery Poll', *The Financial Times*, 10 July 1995.

privatised and in a form which allows the public to express its preferences directly? This need not entail turning museums and galleries run on bureaucratic lines into profit-making private enterprises. They could be operated as non-profit-making institutions, though required to cover their long-run costs more along the lines of the National Trusts, qualified by the public participation measures outlined above. Exceptions could be made in the case of palaces and national monuments which would continue in state ownership, though the running of such institutions could be turned over to franchised private agencies. They could be given freedom to price their services and to raise funds from subscribers and sponsors, within the self-financing constraint.

Externalities of consumption could be regained by a provision of grants or vouchers to enable targeted groups of individuals to meet entry charges – though this need not prevent museum and gallery management from instituting special rates or free days. Research and training costs could be met from government grants, provided these were separately identified. The freedom to de-accession could be coupled with a provision that, in cases where the institution was subject to the guidelines of a sustainable heritage policy, sales could be used only to finance substitute artefacts. Consistent with these guidelines, owners of historic buildings should be given much more freedom to adapt and extend them both to accord with demand for space, domestic or commercial, and to give more opportunities to architects not merely to act as conservers of past styles but to produce innovations which marry the present to the past. After all, there are copious examples, notably in the case of the English cathedrals and historic homes, in which the evolution and mixture of styles represent their appeal to professionals and the untutored alike.

One can sympathise with those who are in the 'heritage business' who would be faced by an intense cultural shock if an approach to its financing followed these recommendations for, unlike privatised public utilities, they have little experience of a régime in which those who enjoy their services have the power to influence what is offered them. The resolute opposition to charging, for example, has assumed the guise of a moral crusade against the 'infidel' (the Treasury) and those state museums and galleries which have introduced charges justify them largely on the grounds of evil necessity. When asked to reply to Brian Sewell (see above, p. 18), the V&A Museum declined to do so, and the poor 'victim' from a national museum who was induced to explain why charges were necessary only agreed if he (or she) could remain anonymous![23] One hopes that a sensible dialogue can take place so that at least the issues of financing can be properly addressed. As I have stated elsewhere:

> '[I]f the public at large are to be treated as passive adjusters to heritage services which are pre-ordained by their producers, this [is] inconsistent with the educational mission that the producers themselves believe to be one of their most important functions.'[24]

Instead of fixing their sights on ever-increasing government funding, professional supporters of heritage services should have their minds concentrated on how subsidy policy can be used to achieve its own demise. The true test of the success of professional efforts to expand and improve appreciation of our heritage is the public's willingness to pay from its own pocket.

---

[23] See the unsigned article, 'Charges at what Cost?', in *The Art Quarterly*, The National Art Collections Fund, Autumn 1997, pp.15-16.

[24] See Alan Peacock, British Academy Keynes Lecture, *op. cit.*, p.220.

2

PUBLIC CHOICE, COST-BENEFIT

ANALYSIS, AND THE EVALUATION OF

CULTURAL HERITAGE

Bruno S. Frey*

University of Zurich

and

Felix Oberholzer-Gee

Wharton School, University of Pennsylvania

1. Introduction

EVERYONE AGREES THAT WE SHOULD PROTECT OUR
CULTURAL HERITAGE. Monuments, groups of buildings and
moveable cultural property such as paintings, drawings and
antiquities are generally taken to be worth preserving if they
'represent a unique artistic achievement' and 'meet the test of
authenticity'.[1] While principles such as the ones stated in the World
Heritage Convention form a convenient basis for noble speeches of
all sorts, they do not provide much guidance for practical public
policy decisions on the preservation of our cultural heritage.
Governments and public administrators face three difficult questions
when making such policy decisions: When should governments
intervene in real estate and art markets in order to 'correct' market

* The financial support of the Swiss National Fund (project 12-42480.94) is gratefully
acknowledged.

[1] UNESCO, *Convention Concerning the Protection of the World Cultural Heritage*, Paris:
UNESCO, 1972.

outcomes? What portion of the overall budget should be allocated to the conservation of our cultural heritage? And, given limited financial means, which among the many monuments, buildings and paintings should be preserved?

The answers to all three questions depend on the social value of preservation efforts. Maintaining the stock of cultural objects creates opportunity costs because the resources involved (labour, material inputs and, especially in the case of monuments, valuable land) could be used for alternative purposes. These costs have to be compared with the benefits that accrue to society if the cultural heritage is protected and preserved. Given the nature of the problem, cost-benefit analysis provides a useful framework which allows policy-makers to analyse systematically the effects of conservation programmes. The British Department of National Heritage and many other public administrations thus employ cost-benefit analysis (and cost-utility analysis for smaller projects) to evaluate all proposals for expenditure.[2]

Assessing the cost side of conservation efforts is a straightforward exercise. Most of the inputs are traded in fairly competitive markets. Market prices thus reflect the social value of these resources. In contrast, it is much more difficult to compute the benefits of conservation since these typically include intangible values. Economic theory offers a wide range of approaches and techniques that may help to compute the benefits of financial support for the arts and historic preservation. The goal is to assess how much value individuals derive from these policies. Their willingness-to-pay is, therefore, investigated.

Section 2 of this chapter discusses various methods designed to estimate the benefits of public conservation policies. More specifically, we will analyse the strengths and weaknesses of the contingent valuation method which many analysts now employ. Section 3

---

[2] S. Creigh-Tyte, P. Daffern, M. Davies and G. Siddorn, *Option Appraisal of Expenditure Decisions: A Guide for the Department of National Heritage and Its Non-Departmental Public Bodies*, London: Department of National Heritage, 1996; N. Lichfield, *Economics in Urban Conservation*, Cambridge: Cambridge University Press: 1988, pp. 240-48.

Cost utility analyses relate budgetary cost to several benefit measures. This type of analysis, originally developed to evaluate health policies, is mostly used to assess the relative advantages of some projects over others. In most cases, cost-utility analyses consider only budgetary costs and fail to consider all social costs. See K. Gerard, 'Cost-Utility in Practice: A Policy Maker's Guide to the State of the Art', *Health Policy*, Vol. 21(3), 1992, pp. 249-79.

presents an alternative policy approach which fundamentally differs from the social welfare considerations underlying the willingness-to-pay studies. It is based on constitutional choice and proposes to integrate the evaluation and the decision on historic preservation programmes by using direct democratic institutions. Section 4 compares this alternative approach to the likely outcomes under expert-based decision-making procedures. Section 5 offers conclusions.

2. Evaluation Procedures

Many cities seek to revive their centres and attract new businesses, residents and tourists by conducting urban renewal programmes. The restoration and conservation of historic monuments and groups of buildings as well as the opening and refurbishing of art institutions (museums, concert halls) is an important part of these policies.[3] As the threshold of historical significance creeps forward and urban renewal policies gain in momentum, the number of listed buildings and monuments steadily increases. In the UK alone, half-a-million buildings are currently listed. More than 8,000 conservation areas are protected by law.[4]

Everyone agrees that the restoration of historic buildings represents an important part of urban renewal strategies. But there is little systematic knowledge about the tastes and preferences of the prospective residents and tourists these policy initiatives are designed to attract. Some studies indicate that familiarity with historic townscapes plays a decisive rôle: people prefer what they know.[5] Other researchers, however, observe that buildings are found attractive if they are moderately novel, and that both very familiar and very progressive projects fail to find much acclaim.[6] In general, there is little evidence that people view architecture as

---

[3] G. J. Ashworth and J. E. Tunbridge, *The Tourist-Historic City*, London: Belhaven, 1990.

[4] P. Hubbard, 'The Value of Conservation: A Critical Review of Behavioural Research', *Town Planning Review*, Vol. 64(4), 1993, pp. 359-73.

[5] J. L. Nasar, 'The Influence of Familiarity on Responses to Visual Quality of Neighborhoods', *Perceptual and Motor Skills*, Vol. 51(2), 1980, pp. 635-42.

[6] T. R. Herzog, R. Kaplan and S. Kaplan, 'The Prediction of Preference for Familiar Urban Places', *Environment and Behaviour*, Vol. 8(4), 1976, pp. 627-41.

historic documents and wish to maintain buildings just because they are old.[7]

With no general theory at hand, policy-makers and cost-benefit analysts have to rely on case studies to determine the size of the benefits associated with programmes that support the arts and historic preservation.[8] To compute these benefits represents a formidable challenge because investments in art and good architecture, it is argued, produce positive externalities.[9] Good architecture is not only enjoyed by the owner of a well-preserved house, but also by passers-by. However, the latter do not pay for the pleasure of strolling in an historically interesting townscape. Similarly, our cultural heritage creates a sense of belonging and group identity which many people value.[10] For example, no fewer than 14 local pressure groups sought to prevent the demolition of three 19th-century buildings in the Rittenhouse Square of Philadelphia, not so much because they were interested in the historic value of these buildings but because the groups felt that they were defending their way of life.[11] However, as is the case with good architecture, everyone may reap the benefits of such group activities which foster identity, irrespective of their own (costly) contributions. Consequently, individuals have a powerful incentive to free-ride, and market prices do not reflect the full social value of art and historic buildings. As a result, society underinvests in these

---

[7] For a review of these issues, see P. Hubbard, 'The Value of Conservation: A Critical Review of Behavioural Research', *Town Planning Review*, Vol. 64(4), 1993, pp. 359-73.

[8] Examples of such case studies include the economic appraisal of the Horniman Museum in S. Creigh-Tyte, P. Daffern, M. Davies and G. Siddorn, *Option Appraisal of Expenditure Decisions: A Guide for the Department of National Heritage and Its Non-Departmental Public Bodies,op.cit.*, 1996, pp. 56-70. Lichfield also presents a number of cases: N. Lichfield, *Economics in Urban Conservation, op. cit.*, Ch. 16, pp. 289-314.

[9] B. S. Frey and W. W. Pommerehne, *Muses and Markets: Explorations in the Economics of Art*, Oxford: Blackwell, 1990; G. Allison, S. Ball, P. Cheshire, A. Evans and M. Stabler, *The Value of Conservation: A Literature Review of the Economic and Social Value of the Cultural Built Heritage*, London: The Department of National Heritage, English Heritage, and The Royal Institution of Chartered Surveyors, 1996.

[10] S. M. Taylor and V. A. Konrad, 'Scaling Dispositions to the Past', *Environment and Behaviour*, Vol. 12(3), 1980, pp. 283-307.

[11] S. C. Bourassa, *The Aesthetics of Landscape*, London: Belhaven Press, 1991.

goods, and government programmes to correct this market failure may be warranted. The assessment of tangible and intangible benefits in cost-benefit analyses is thus essential: if positive externalities exist, government interventions can be justified. Otherwise, the conservation of our cultural heritage should be left to the market. Where government intervenes to preserve historic buildings or subsidise art institutions, cost-benefit analyses produce a systematic ranking of possible projects according to the size of their net present value. There are at least three well-established methods to assess the individual willingness-to-pay for non-market goods:[12] (i) the hedonic pricing approach; (ii) the travel cost method; and (iii) contingent valuation. We will discuss these in turn and analyse to what extent they may be suitable for a cost-benefit analysis of historic conservation efforts.

(i) Hedonic Pricing

The hedonic pricing method analyses how specific attributes of goods are valued.[13] For example, the analyst compares the prices of houses which differ in their characteristics (age, number of bedrooms, distance from city centre). Using regression analysis, it is possible to determine how house prices vary with changes in each of these characteristics. The characteristics may include amenities and 'house properties' that are not directly traded in markets, such as clean air, noise from an airport or the distance to a landfill. For example, Nelson *et al.* (1992) have shown that, keeping all other characteristics constant, house prices decline by 6 per cent if homes are located within a mile of a landfill in Minnesota.[14]

Using the hedonic pricing method, a number of studies have attempted to determine the price effects of architectural styles, historic conservation and listing on property values. In their

---

[12] W. W. Pommerehne, *Präferenzen für öffentliche Güter: Ansätze zu ihrer Erfassung*, Tübingen: Mohr (Siebeck), 1987; E. M. Gramlich, *A Guide to Benefit-Cost Analysis*, Englewood Cliffs, N.J.: Prentice Hall, 1990.

[13] K. Lancaster, *Consumer Demand:A New Approach*, New York: Columbia University Press, 1971; S. Rosen, 'Hedonic Prices and Implicit Markets: Product Differentiation in Pure Competition', *Journal of Political Economy*, Vol. 82(1), 1974, pp. 34-55.

[14] A. C. Nelson, J. Genereux and M. Genereux, 'Price Effects of Landfills on House Values', *Land Economics*, Vol. 68(4), 1992, pp. 359-65.

analysis of 19th-century row houses (called terraced houses in Britain) in Boston, Moorhouse and Smith (1994) show that architectural styles systematically influence the willingness-to-pay for these homes.[15] Compared to the dominant Italianate style, home-owners are prepared to pay a premium for Neo-Grec homes. In contrast, Renaissance Revival and Victorian Gothic homes trade at a discount. The results of the study generally suggest a high willingness-to-pay for architectural features such as elaborate ornamentation or quoins which distinguish the row house from other buildings in its vicinity. Similarly, Hough and Kratz (1983) report that a considerable premium is paid for office buildings of good architecture in Chicago.[16] This finding, however, applies only to new office buildings that were awarded prizes for architectural excellence, not for older buildings listed as national or Chicago landmarks. The authors attribute this finding to the fact that owners of listed buildings partially lose their property rights. Once a building is listed, it becomes more difficult to renovate and upgrade the building.

Schaeffer and Millerick (1991) confirm this interpretation. Looking at house prices in an historic residential district, they find that property values increased by almost 30 per cent after the area was listed in the National Register of Historic Places.[17] In contrast, the houses in two smaller zones declined in value after they were designated as Chicago Historic Districts. Again, they conclude that the more restrictive Chicago regulations were responsible for this negative effect.

These hedonic pricing studies are valuable because they shed some light on the effects of listing and the nature of individual preferences for architecture. But they fail to capture the full benefits of historic preservation as is necessary to determine whether government intervention is warranted. And they do not produce unbiased estimates of the net present value of conservation

---

[15] J. C. Moorhouse and M. S. Smith, 'The Market for Residential Architecture: 19th Century Row Houses in Boston's South End', *Journal of Urban Economics*, Vol. 35, 1994, pp. 267-77.

[16] D. E. Hough and C. G. Kratz, 'Can "Good" Architecture Meet the Market Test?', *Journal of Urban Economics*, Vol. 14, 1983, pp. 40-54.

[17] P. V. Schaeffer and C. A. Millerick, 'The Impact of Historic District Designation on Property Values: An Empirical Study', *Economic Development Quarterly*, Vol. 5(4), 1991, pp. 301-12.

efforts. On the demand side, hedonic pricing does not capture the value of the public good characteristics of good architecture. Since a building's appeal is not only available to the owners or the tenants, but also to neighbours and tourists, hedonic pricing estimates are biased downwards. On the supply side, owners may value the fact that they rent out a building of historic value. Where this is the case, they earn not only a financial but also a psychic return. However, in market equilibrium, the sum of these returns will not exceed the market return. Therefore, rents such as the ones studied by Hough and Kratz (1983) understate the true social value of good architecture.

(ii) Travel Cost Method

The travel cost approach is based on the clever insight that individuals reveal their willingness-to-pay to see a monument or visit a museum if they bear the cost of travelling to the site.[18] The analyst thus surveys visitors in order to determine where they came from, how much they had to spend to travel to the site of interest, and how often they plan to visit it. This information can be used to estimate a demand curve and the related social surplus associated with the monument.[19]   As the implied value is measured by the (travel) cost individuals are prepared to incur to visit a particular cultural site, this method gives a lower bound estimate; it is quite possible that a visit yields much higher benefits than the cost incurred. Moreover, the travel cost method suffers from three other difficulties.

For most trips, travelling time makes up a significant portion of the overall travel cost. Most economic studies have used the going market wage as a proxy for the value of time. However, the relationship between market wages and the value of time is ambiguous.[20]   If individuals experience some disutility from job

---

[18] The method is attributed to H. Hotelling, 'Letter': *An Economic Study of the Monetary Evaluation of Recreation in the National Parks*, Washington, DC: National Park Service, 1949.

[19] For the evaluation of specific characteristics of a site, see G. Brown and R. Mendelsohn, 'The Hedonic Travel Cost Model', *Review of Economics and Statistics*, Vol. 66(3), 1984, pp. 427-33.

[20] J. R. McKean, D. M. Johnson and R. G. Walsh, 'Valuing Time in Travel Cost Demand Analysis: An Empirical Investigation', *Land Economics*, Vol. 71(1), 1995, pp. 96-105.

activities, their market wage does not only represent a compensation for the value of time. Therefore, the value of time should be lower than going market wages. On the other hand, some individuals enjoy working (they have a substantial intrinsic work motivation), which should be reflected in a value of time higher than the going wage rate. In fact, revealed-preference studies sometimes suggest that individuals attach higher values to leisure than is implied by their market wages.[21] The issue gets even more complicated if one recognises that, under certain circumstances, the trip itself may yield pleasure. In this case, the monetary travel costs overestimate the true willingness-to-pay. As a consequence, it is not at all clear how one should value one of the major cost components of any travel cost study.

Multipurpose trips represent a further difficulty. Individuals will typically not be able to tell the analyst what portion of the overall travel cost they bear because they wanted to see the Colosseum, and what fraction they spent to walk on the Forum Romanum. For isolated sites, it may be possible to identify individuals who had several reasons to visit a site. In the case of cities, however, this method would lead to the exclusion of virtually all the visitors.

A further difficulty of the travel cost method relates to substitutes for the sites in question. To produce reliable estimates of the social surplus, the price of substitutes needs to be included in the econometric estimates.[22] However, as individual tastes are not known, it will generally not be possible to determine what monuments, groups of historic buildings or art objects tourists regard as substitutes. Are the Uffici a relevant substitute for the Louvre, or is it the gardens of Versailles? Finally, it may well be that the travel cost variable itself is endogenous to the choice of residence. People may prefer to live in the city because of the vicinity to museums. If this is the case, the number of visits to these museums and the price of the trips are determined simultaneously. Therefore, the travel cost equation cannot be identified and the travel cost variable may not be independent of the error term, leading to biased and inconsistent estimates.

---

[21] R. T. Deacon and J. Sonstelle, 'Rationing by Waiting and the Value of Time: Results from a Natural Experiment', *Journal of Political Economy*, Vol. 93(4), 1985, pp. 627-47.

[22] V. K. Smith and Y. Kaoru, 'Signals or Noise? Explaining the Variation in Recreation Benefit Estimates', *American Journal of Agricultural Economics*, May 1990, pp. 419-33.

(iii) Contingent Valuation

In a contingent valuation (CV) study, individuals are asked to state their maximum willingness-to-pay to preserve an art object or an historic monument. Alternatively, respondents are sometimes given a fixed price that secures the conservation of a monument. They can then decide whether they are willing to pay the suggested price. This latter method is known as the dichotomous choice approach or the referendum format. In both cases, CV researchers use the individual answers to construct an aggregate demand curve and to compute the social surplus of conserving a monument.

CV studies are superior to hedonic pricing and travel cost estimates in that they are able to capture the 'non-use values' of the art institutions and historic monuments.[23] These non-use values consist of existence, option and bequest values. By taking non-use values into account, analysts recognise that some individuals derive benefits from the mere knowledge that a place exists or that they or their children may be able to visit it at some time in the future. The CV method is now widely used by economists. A recent study sponsored by the Royal Institution of Chartered Surveyors, English Heritage, and the Department of National Heritage concludes that, 'in an urban context, systematic Contingent Valuation Method research ... would be the most useful' of the valuation approaches currently available.[24]

Over the years, considerable experience with CV studies has been gained. In their bibliography, Carson *et al.* (1994) list almost 1,700 studies in over 40 countries.[25] Early examples include evaluations of a reduction in household soiling and cleaning,[26] the right to hunt waterfowl,[27] reduced congestion in wilderness areas,[28] and improved

---

[23] P. R. Portney, 'The Contingent Valuation Debate: Why Economists Should Care', *Journal of Economic Perspectives*, Vol. 8(4), 1994, pp. 3-17.

[24] G. Allison, S. Ball, P. Cheshire, A. Evans and M. Stabler, *op. cit.*, p.21.

[25] R. Carson *et al.*, *A Bibliography of Contingent Valuation Studies and Papers*, La Jolla, California: Natural Resources Damage Assessment, Inc., 1994.

[26] R. Ridker, *The Economic Cost of Air Pollution*, New York: Praeger, 1967.

[27] J. Hammack and G. Brown, *Waterfowl and Wetlands: Toward Bioeconomic Analysis*, Amsterdam: North Holland, 1974.

[28] C. J. Cicchetti and V. K. Smith, 'Congestion, Quality Deterioration, and Optimal Use:

air visibility.[29] Most CV studies evaluate objects in the natural environment. But there are other applications, such as the reduced risk of dying from heart attack,[30] reduced risk of respiratory disease,[31] and even improved information about grocery store prices.[32]

Although the method is now widely used, many economists remain sceptical because surveys do not rely on observed choices (revealed preferences), but on hypothetical answers.[33] Consequently, it is costless for individuals to distort their preferences and give strategic answers. This concern became especially important in a recent application which attempted to measure the environmental damage caused by the supertanker *Exxon Valdez* which ran aground in Prince William Sound, Alaska, spilling 11 million gallons of crude oil into the sea.[34] The enormous sums of money involved in the litigation connected with the Alaskan oil spill has further drawn the attention of the economics community to the contingent valuation method. Well-known economists have been employed as advisers by public authorities, environmental interest groups, and by the oil company. As a consequence, the contingent valuation method has come under careful scrutiny.

Wilderness Recreation in the Spanish Peaks Primitive Area', *Social Science Research*, Vol. 2, 1973, pp. 15-30.

[29] A. Randall, B. C. Ives, and C. Eastman, 'Bidding Games for Valuation of Aesthetic Environmental Improvements', *Journal of Environmental Economics and Management*, Vol. 1, 1974, pp. 132-49.

[30] J. Acton, *Evaluating Public Progress to Save Lives: The Case of Heart Attacks*, RAND Research Report R-73-02, Santa Monica: RAND Corporation, 1973.

[31] A. Krupnick and M. Cropper, 'The Effect of Information on Health Risk Valuation', *Journal of Risk and Uncertainty*, Vol. 2, 1992, pp. 29-48.

[32] D. G. Devine and B. Marion, 'The Influence of Consumer Price Information on Retail Pricing and Consumer Behaviour', *American Journal of Agricultural Economics*, Vol. 61 (May), 1979, pp. 228-37.

[33] P. A. Diamond and J. A. Hausman, 'Contingent Valuation: Is Some Number Better than No Number?', *Journal of Economic Perspectives*, Vol. 8(4), 1994, pp. 45-64.

[34] R. Carson *et al.*, *A Contingent Valuation Study of Lost Passive Use Values Resulting From the Exxon Valdez Oil Spill*, Report to the Attorney General of the State of Alaska prepared by Natural Resource Damage Assessment, Inc., La Jolla, California, 1992.

The United States National Oceanic and Atmospheric Administration (NOAA) hired two Nobel prize winners (Professors Kenneth Arrow and Robert Solow) to co-chair a panel (including Edward Leamer, Roy Radner, Paul Portney and Howard Schuman, a professor of sociology and survey research expert) with the task of assessing the CV method. The bottom line of the panel report concludes that 'CV studies can produce estimates reliable enough to be the starting point of a judicial process of damage assessment, including lost passive-use values'.[35] The term 'passive-use values' refers to the non-use values of the environment mentioned above. While the report generally endorsed the use of CV methods, it also stated a large number of stringent requirements for that conclusion to hold. The most important are:

- personal interviews rather than telephone surveys should be conducted;

- an accurate description of the expected effects of the programme under consideration must be given;

- the budget constraint must be well specified; and

- the respondents must be reminded of the substitutes for the commodity in question.

However, even in cases where these requirements are all met, CV estimates appear to produce results that are inconsistent with market choices. In a recent experiment, only one-half of respondents who had indicated earlier that they would be willing to purchase a juicer (the CV question) were later willing actually to purchase the appliance when given this choice.[36] The referendum format used in this experiment is certainly preferable to maximum willingness-to-pay questions because consumers are much more familiar with dichotomous choices. However, even these formats do not appear always to produce reliable estimates.

---

[35] K. J. Arrow, R. S. Solow, E. Leamer, P. Portney, R. Radner and H. Schuman, 'Report of the NOAA-Panel on Contingent Valuation', *Federal Register*, Vol. 58(10), 1993, pp. 4,601-14.

[36] R. G. Cummings, G. W. Harrison and E. E. Rutström, 'Homegrown Values and Hypothetical Surveys: Is the Dichotomous Choice Approach Incentive-Compatible?', *American Economic Review*, Vol. 85(1), 1995, pp. 260-66.

Recently, Sen presented an additional, and even more fundamental, critique that questions the way CV results are to be interpreted.[37] In particular, he raises some issues concerning the social choice assumptions that underlie the CV approach. The CV method imitates the purchase and consumption of a private good. It thus presumes that the benefits from the project in question can be achieved single-handedly. In the case of the Alaskan oil spill, for example, a respondent is asked how much she would pay to save the birds that perished. If she answers £32, this answer is interpreted to mean that this individual is prepared to make a payment of £32 in order to wipe out *all the losses* from the perished birds. Sen argues that 'it is hard to imagine that this question and answer can be taken seriously, since the state of affairs the person is asked to imagine could not possibly be true'. On the contrary, if the person actually believed that a single payment of £32 could clear up all the damage, this would constitute an extreme form of irrationality. But if people were irrational, the whole approach of asking individuals to evaluate a good would be mistaken.

As our example makes clear, the contingent valuation procedure only makes sense when it is constructed to reach a policy goal by a joint effort. An individual's payment is a contribution to that end. If one interprets the question about one's willingness-to-pay as a contribution to a joint effort, a new problem arises because a respondent's stated sum now depends on how much she expects others to contribute. There are two opposing effects at work. If a respondent is willing to contribute provided that others also join the effort, the incentive structure of an assurance game results.[38] In contrast, if the respondent feels less pressed to contribute if the others already do, free-riding is the outcome, and the respondents all refuse to state any willingness-to-pay. Depending on whether the scenario favoured the assurance game or the free-riding interpretation, the stated sums differ widely. In any case, the individual as well as the aggregate willingness-to-pay are difficult to interpret.

---

[37] A. K. Sen, 'Environmental Evaluation and Social Choice: Contingent Valuation and the Market Analogy', *The Japanese Economic Review*, Vol. 46(1), 1995, pp. 23-37.

[38] A. K. Sen, 'Isolation, Assurance and the Social Rate of Discount', *Quarterly Journal of Economics*, Vol. 81, 1967, pp. 112-24.

These problems and limitations of the contingent valuation method also apply to studies that attempt to measure the value of our cultural heritage. There are but a few studies using the contingent valuation procedure on issues of culture. Some have attempted to measure the broad support for the arts and the level of desired government expenditures.[39] Bille Hansen (1995) uses the CV method to value the Royal Danish Opera in Copenhagen,[40] and Martin (1994) evaluates the justification of subsidies for the Musée de la Civilisation in Quebec.[41]

Contingent Valuation and Cultural Heritage

In the following, we address two additional problems which are of special importance when contingent valuation is applied to cultural heritage.

(i) Marginal vs. total changes: CV studies typically confront the respondents with an 'all-or-none' choice, or with an indivisible good. Either the villa or the gallery is preserved *in toto*, or not at all. Bille Hansen (1995) explicitly states, for example, that the Royal Danish Theatre is to be run at the *present* activity level. Clearly, it is always possible to vary the level – though that option is routinely and fervently rejected by the suppliers. One possibility would be to give up the ballet section, or the opera section, and the respondents could then be asked their willingness-to-pay for these different activity levels. Even a villa or a gallery could only be partly preserved, without completely destroying the respective historical value. Constructing such a demand curve for various sizes or qualities of the cultural good is, in principle, possible but would involve much additional work.

[39] D. C. Throsby and G. A. Withers, 'Measuring the Demand for the Arts as a Public Good: Theory and Empirical Results', in W. S. Hendon and J. L. Shanahan (eds.), *Economics of Cultural Decisions*, Cambridge, MA.: Abt, 1983, pp. 177-91; W. G. Morrison and E. G. West, 'Subsidies for the Performing Arts: Evidence on Voter Preferences', *Journal of Behavioural Economics*, Vol. 15 (Fall), 1986, pp. 57-72.

[40] B. Hansen, 'A CV Study of Willingness-to-Pay for the Royal Theatre in Copenhagen', *Mimeo*, AKF; Institute of Local Government Studies, Copenhagen, 1995.

[41] F. Martin, 'Determining the Size of Museum Subsidies', *Journal of Cultural Economics*, Vol. 18, 1994, pp. 255-70.

ii) Suboptimal supply: This second issue is closely connected to the first, but is not identical. The contingent valuation method does not include an optimising algorithm, that is, the historic object is presented to the respondents as it is. It is (implicitly) assumed that supply is already efficient. *First*, this means that the art institutions are so perfectly run that no improvement is possible without having to give up some other goal (X-efficiency). This assumption is heroic, to say the least. It is known from the economics of art that large opportunities for improvements in technical efficiency exist.[42] *Second*, CV studies also assume efficiency in the sense that the consumers' preferences are met. Again, art economists provide overwhelming evidence to the contrary. In particular, the directors of theatres, museums but also of historic sites exploit the discretionary room accorded to them to follow their own preferences which systematically and significantly deviate from what the average citizens – who are relevant in willingness-to-pay studies – desire.

We conclude that CV studies promise to yield worthwhile results because they force the researchers to undertake a determined, and extensive, analysis of the art object in question. The questionnaire has to meet stringent requirements to be useful at all. Even more importantly, the representative survey approach addresses both visitors and non-visitors, and it has the potential to capture non-use values. However, it is not clear under what conditions CV estimates can be accepted as reliable estimates for the true willingness-to-pay of individuals. Moreover, the results of CV studies are difficult to interpret if joint efforts are required to produce the public good in question.

Cost-Benefit Analyses

As the previous discussion has shown, all three major methods available for the assessment of our cultural heritage are beset with problems. But even if the value of conservation efforts were known, a number of serious difficulties arise in conducting a cost-benefit analysis to compare the benefits of historic conservation with its cost. We address three important issues, namely,

---

[42] B. S. Frey and W. W. Pommerehne, *op. cit,;* D. C. Throsby, 'The Production and Consumption of the Arts: A View of Cultural Economics', *Journal of Economic Literature,* Vol. 33, 1994, pp. 1-29.

discounting, the distribution of costs and benefits, and theoretical inconsistencies. The benefits of historic conservation extend far into the future while most of the costs are borne by today's taxpayers and parts of the population that are negatively affected by these programmes. This poses two problems. *First*, benefits (and costs) need to be discounted. *Second*, both benefits (and costs) are to some extent uncertain because they extend into the future. As always, economists refer to individual preferences as the yardstick of all valuation. The individual marginal rate of time preference is the appropriate discount rate and option values represent the correct certainty equivalents to uncertain prospects.[43]

However, what is the appropriate discount rate if we observe that the same individuals save at interest rates below 4 per cent and, at one and the same time, accumulate credit card debts on which they pay interest well above 15 per cent?[44] To complicate matters further, theory requires the analyst to convert forgone investment to changes in consumption (by applying the shadow price of capital) before discounting.[45] This approach is sensible because a pound of investment (which creates further consumption possibilities in the future) is more valuable than a pound of consumption. However, as the source of specific budgetary outlays is generally not known, standard practice ignores the distinction between changes in consumption and changes in investment.[46] Similarly, the difference between option prices and expected surplus is generally neglected due to the formidable difficulties in obtaining the necessary data. Given these difficulties, it may not be surprising that a recent survey of 90 large US municipalities found that less than half of them use any discounting procedures at all. And even at the federal level

---

[43] D. A. Graham, 'Cost-Benefit Analysis under Uncertainty', *American Economic Review*, Vol. 71(4), 1981, pp. 715-25.

[44] Reasons for further intertemporal inconsistencies are discussed by G. Loewenstein and D. Prelec, 'Anomalies in Intertemporal Choice: Evidence and an Interpretation', *Quarterly Journal of Economics*, Vol. 197(2), 1992, pp. 573-97.

[45] D. F. Bradford, 'Constraint on Government Investment Opportunities and the Choice of Discount Rate', *American Economic Review*, Vol. 65(5), 1975, pp. 887-99.

[46] A. E. Boardman, D. H. Greenberg, A. R. Vining and D. L. Weimer, *Cost Benefit Analysis: Concepts and Practice*, Upper Saddle River, NJ: Prentice Hall, 1996.

where there are presumably many economists engaged in the respective studies, different US agencies use widely differing discounting approaches.[47] 'One thousand points of light seeking a number,' is how the director of the Congressional Budget Office, Robert W. Hartman, aptly described the search for the appropriate discount rate.[48]

The distribution of costs and benefits which results from historic preservation programmes is arguably even more important than questions of discounting. Large-scale efforts of city renewal often lead to the gentrification of the targeted areas and displace low-income groups. In addition, many residents fear the 'museumisation' which conservation areas often produce, killing the life in these neighbourhoods and destroying the original social fabric. Therefore, targeted areas frequently resist ambitious plans for restoration. The French system of *secteurs sauvegardés,* introduced by the 1962 Malraux Act, provides a good example for the social tensions conservation efforts can produce. The French law, which served as a model for the Italian urban conservation system and the British 1967 Civic Amenities act, concentrated public expenditure on small areas that were to be thoroughly conserved. For example, the planners intended to return the Marais in Paris to the exact form shown on the Turgot plan of 1739. All 19th-century 'accretions' were to be stripped away. However, local councils blocked the approval for this particular and many other plans. For most safeguarded zones it took more than a decade to win local approval and the majority of plans is still blocked.[49] From this point of view, the Malraux Act must be judged a failure because it did not consider the distributional consequences of historic conservation.

The distributional consequences of preservation programmes are clearly very important. However, cost-benefit and cost-utility

---

[47] R. M. Lyon, 'Federal Discount Rate Policy, the Shadow Price of Capital, and Challenges for Reforms', *Journal of Environmental Economics and Management,* Vol. 18(2), 1990, pp. S29-S50.

[48] R. W. Hartman, 'One Thousand Points of Light Seeking a Number: A Case Study of CBO's Search for a Discount Policy', *Journal of Environmental Economics and Manage-ment,* Vol. 18(2), 1990, pp. S3-S7.

[49] R. Kain, 'Europe's Model and Exemplar Still? The French Approach to Urban Conservation, 1962-1981', *Town Planning Review,* Vol. 53, 1982, pp. 403-22.

analyses have nothing to say about the distribution of costs and benefits. Policies can be ranked according to the size of their net present values, indicating the gains in overall resources to society. The distribution of these resources, however, is beyond the realm of cost-benefit analysis. In fact, policies that make the urban poor even poorer are perfectly compatible with the Kaldor/Hicks compensation principle[50] by which cost-benefit analysts judge subsidies for the arts and conservation efforts. It has been suggested that this shortcoming of cost-benefit analysis could be remedied by weighting the losses to the poor more heavily than the gains to the middle classes and the rich.[51] To the extent that increases in income yield diminishing marginal benefits or if citizens have a preference for a more equal distribution of wealth, the use of distributional weights is compatible with economic theory.[52] However, both variables are not directly observable and neither economic theory nor legal stipulations offers any guidance with regard to the numerical values that should be placed on such weights.[53] Therefore, distributional issues remain neglected in practical cost-benefit analyses.

Finally, under certain circumstances, cost-benefit analysis may make contradictory recommendations because the method is unable to rank different Pareto-superior states.[54] In these cases, the cost-benefit analyst recommends undertaking the proposed historic preservation and compensating the losers, and he also recommends not having the programme and compensating the groups that would have gained from preserving our cultural heritage. Both policies represent net improvements in overall welfare and the logic of cost-benefit analysis implies that both programmes should be undertaken – which is not possible as the recommendations are contradictory.

---

[50] The principle that a policy should be undertaken if the winners *could* compensate the losers and still remain better off.

[51] A. C. Harberger, 'On the Use of Distributional Weights in Social Cost-Benefit Analysis', *Journal of Political Economy*, Vol. 86(2), 1978, pp. 87-120.

[52] M. S. Feldstein, 'Distributional Equity and the Optimal Structure of Public Prices', *American Economic Review*, Vol. 62(1), 1972, pp. 32-36.

[53] N. Lichfield, *Community Impact Evaluation*, London: University College London, 1996, pp. 260-71.

[54] States in which at least one player has become better off without anyone becoming worse off.

3. Combining Evaluation and Decision by Referenda

The evaluation methods currently available, and cost-benefit analyses as a conceptual framework, are of limited use for public policy purposes. They do not provide a coherent framework which could serve as the basis for rational public conservation decisions. Moreover, the cost-benefit approach fails to take distributive aspects of these policies into account. The last aspect is of particular importance because these conservation decisions are taken in the realm of politics where distributive effects are more important than allocative efficiency. Thus, the major problem with willingness-to-pay studies which are based on social welfare considerations is that they are divorced from political decisions. These methods are of little importance in the political process because they exclusively (attempt to) relate to social welfare and ignore political exigencies. Some actors may under some circumstances use the results of cost-benefit studies to bolster their arguments – provided they suit their interests.

To overcome the problems discussed in Section 2, we propose to reveal the individual willingness-to-pay for the conservation of our cultural heritage by holding popular referenda on questions of preservation and allowing initiatives. As the NOAA panel had pointed out, a well-designed contingent valuation study seeks to imitate a popular referendum – why, then, should it not be employed? As a decision mechanism, referenda have many advantages over representative and administrative forms of decision-making. In particular, referenda evade the principal-agent problem and constitute an effective barrier against the *'classe politique'*. Both aspects are of particular importance with respect to cultural decisions because the politicians and bureaucrats tend to have a larger discretionary room in this area than elsewhere.

We consider the following three forms of public participation in conservation planning and public policies related to our cultural heritage:

- Citizens should be granted the right to vote on the size of the overall budget for the arts and for historic preservation (budget referenda).

- Citizens also have the right to approve or reject large projects such as the construction of a new museum (project referenda).

- Citizens may propose new laws with regard to the arts or introduce new conservation projects (initiatives).

These three forms of public participation are designed to bring heritage policies as close to individual preferences as possible. However, it is also important to recognise the gains in efficiency that result from the division of labour between politicians, preservation experts and the public at large. Therefore, we propose to leave the traditional budget process unchanged. Administrators and politicians know best how to work out the intricate details of a public budget and it is their mandate to propose policies that further the public interest. But, once the budget planning process is concluded, the public should have the right to challenge the proposed budget in a referendum. The mere possibility of challenging the budget in a referendum changes the incentives for all those involved in its preparation. Administrators and politicians now have to anticipate the public's reaction to different proposals and consider the distributional aspects of the proposed policies. The same considerations also hold for project proposals that are subject to public approval.

Most states which use popular referenda require that a fixed number of voters demand a referendum within a few months after the publication of the budget or the project proposal. The hurdle for starting a referendum should neither be set too low nor too high. If too high, the referendum obviously fails to produce the set of incentives that requires administrators and politicians to act in the interests of their constituencies. But it should also not be too easy to start a referendum. Citizens must have the opportunity to collect and process the information on the issues at hand. This is only possible if the number of topics that citizens vote on remains comparatively small. Thus it would be impractical if citizens had to decide on the renovation of every facade in their town. If politicians and administrators correctly anticipate the public's sentiments, we would not expect to see a large number of referenda taking place. The fact that public policy decisions have to take individual preferences into account (without voting actually taking place) represents by far the most important effect of this form of public involvement.

Budget and project referenda reduce the principal-agent problem, but they do not eliminate the agenda-setting power of politicians.

Public policy will become even more efficient if there is increased competition for new ideas. Initiatives which allow citizens to propose and vote on new ideas and projects serve this very purpose. Initiatives open up the political process and let insiders (elected officials and administrators) compete with outsiders (new political entrepreneurs and under-represented groups). Again, one has to think carefully about the requirements for starting an initiative as it is not feasible that citizens be required to vote on every issue.

Arguments against Popular Referenda

Two arguments are often raised against the use of popular referenda for cultural policy.

(i) Incapable citizens: Voters are charged with being both uninformed and unintelligent with respect to cultural affairs. Therefore, they cannot be trusted to take 'good' decisions. The criticism concerning the lack of information is mistaken. When citizens are given the power to decide, they will inform themselves. Today, they do not acquire much information as they cannot decide anything. The state of information is not given, but is endogenous to the political process. The discussion process induced by the referendum produces the necessary information. With respect to the lack of intelligence in matters of historic conservation, referenda rely on the same value-judgement as all other willingness-to-pay methods. In all cases, individual preferences – and not the (supposedly) superior insights of a cultural/political élite – are to count.

(ii) Superficial citizens: Voters are charged with not taking referendum decisions seriously. It is quite true that these decisions are of the 'low-cost' type because a single vote is never decisive. Consequently, the opportunity cost of misrepresenting one's preferences at the polls is low.[55] This charge applies equally to CV procedures, but not to the travel cost method or hedonic pricing which examine revealed behaviour. One may even argue that individuals take a response to a survey more lightly than voting

---

[55] H. Kliemt, 'The Veil of Insignificance', *European Journal of Political Economy*, Vol. 2/3, 1986, pp. 333-44; G. Kirchgässner and W. W. Pommerehne, 'Low-cost decisions as a challenge to public choice', *Public Choice*, Vol. 77 (September), 1993, pp. 107-15.

decisions because the situation is purely hypothetical. Even more importantly, issues put to a referendum are often publicly debated.[56] In these discussions, having an opinion may be of considerable value.[57] Quite often, individuals are looked down upon by their peers if they are not in a position to debate an issue. Such social pressures generate additional incentives to gather and process information on the issue at hand.

4. Democratic Heritage Policies

When discussing public choice aspects of conservation policies, we asserted that decisions taken in the political realm closely mirror their distributional consequences. This applies to our proposal as well. This section compares the referendum approach to the likely outcomes under expert-based decision-making procedures that characterise much of today's arts and preservation policies. By identifying the losers and the winners of the expected changes we hope to gain some insight into the likelihood of political change.

Figure 1 sketches the demand for the public good aspects of historic preservation. This (non-market) demand side is characterised by a bimodal distribution of preference intensities: one group of people treasures the arts and historic conservation and exhibits a high willingness-to-pay for these public goods. A much larger group values our cultural heritage, but is not willing to spend much on its preservation. To simplify the diagrammatic exposition, the demand schedules of only three individuals are shown: one art-lover and two citizens with a smaller willingness-to-pay for the arts. We further simplify the situation by assuming that they all face the same tax prices.

A benevolent dictator would choose the provision of public goods equal to Q* where the vertical sum of the demand for historic conservation is equal to the social costs denoted by the supply curve. This is the point cost-benefit analysts seek to determine if they attempt to measure the individual willingness-to-pay for the arts. In contrast, the median voter is decisive for the outcome in a referendum on historic preservation. Therefore, referendum-

---

[56] B. S. Frey, 'Direct Democracy: Politico-Economic Lessons from Swiss Experience', *American Economic Review*, Vol. 84 (May), 1994, pp. 338-48.

[57] A. O. Hirschman, 'Having Opinions - One of the Elements of Well-Being?', *American Economic Review*, Vol. 79(2), 1989, pp. 75-79.

Figure 1: The Demand for the Public Good Aspects of Historic Preservation

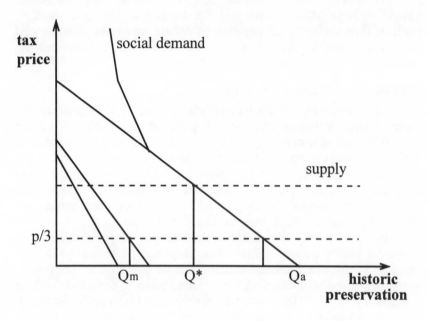

determined supply is equal to Q_m. Compared to the socially optimal provision of art subsidies and historic preservation, referendum processes could lead to an underprovision of public goods. However, this analysis is incomplete. The benevolent social dictator does not exist and one has to compare the outcome of a referendum with decisions made by public administrators.

It is not difficult to foresee who the experts are in a system which gives much weight to expert-driven decisions. Individuals who truly love the arts and have much interest in historic preservation study these subjects and are thus more likely to end up in positions where they can influence public policy. The likely outcome of expert-driven systems is thus in the vicinity of Q_a. Public policies reflect the tastes of the expert community and an overprovision of public goods is likely to result.

Past conservation programmes offer ample evidence for the fact that conservation experts often wish to go further than a balance of marginal costs and benefits would indicate. As mentioned above, in the 1960s and the early 1970s, French and Italian preservation efforts were concentrated on a few small areas. The goal was to restore a small number of zones to perfection.[58]   However, if conservation efforts exhibit increasing marginal costs and decreasing marginal benefits, the funds could have been used with greater effect if more zones had been restored in a less-than-perfect manner.

Similarly, many conservation experts continue to criticise the 'facadist' approach taken by commercial developers and several cities. Instead of restoring houses to historic purity, these development programmes often restore only the facades of buildings. One disputed case is the city of Bristol's decision to replace two Victorian warehouses by early 18th-century Georgian facsimiles, thereby increasing the visual coherence of Queen Square, but removing important historical traces. Predictably, this decision has drawn much criticism from conservation officers and experts.[59]   The debate on facadism clearly shows the differences between the economic approach to historic conservation and the standards of the expert community. If the facades of buildings produce the positive externalities associated with good architecture, economic theory recommends restoring the facades only. Historic conservation is not seen as an end in itself, but rather as a means to convey pleasure. If this goal can be reached without restoring historic buildings in their entirety, the facadist approach is more efficient. In addition, the lack of a premium for older historic office buildings in Chicago and the negative effects of listing on house prices if the regulations are very strict, both indicate that restrictions on changes to the interior are costly. From the economic point of view, the facadist approach thus offers the best of two worlds. Restored facades capture most of the positive externalities without placing a heavy burden on the use of historic buildings.

The comparison between representative decision-making and the constitutional approach that we champion yields the following result: expert-based decision-making tends to lead to the

---

58 R. Kain (1982), *op.cit.*

59 J. V. Punter, 'The Long-term Conservation Programme in Central Bristol 1977-1990', *Town Planning Review,* Vol. 62(3), 1991, pp. 341-64.

overprovision of historic conservation and art subsidies. Most likely, the expenditures will be more heavily concentrated, producing fewer but more prestigious projects. In contrast, decision-making by referenda may lead to an underprovision of public goods because art-lovers are not able to express the intensity of their preferences at the polls.[60]

Lessening Negative Impacts of Referenda

The choice of political institutions thus entails a trade-off between the advantages and disadvantages of expert-based representative and direct-democratic procedures. We believe that the following four mechanisms serve to lessen the negative impacts of referenda and initiatives on conservation policies.

- Not all citizens will vote in a referendum on, say, the conservation budget of a city. Those who do not care about conservation are less likely to participate in the referendum. Moreover, conservation budgets are generally too small to stir major fiscal debates. Consequently, the electorate will consist of disproportionately many 'art-lovers'. Changes in turn-out rates capture preference intensities to some extent. In the cases studied here, they will increase the budget for historic conservation and the arts.

- In referenda, the interest groups and parties seek to affect the vote by newspaper, radio and television campaigns. But an open society admits propaganda from all sides, and it is therefore not *a priori* clear what the effect is. Normally, the cultural interests are well organised and motivated, emanating from the highly subsidised cultural institutions such as museums, theatres, orchestras and other arts organisations. The individuals uninterested or opposed to art belong on average to the less-educated classes of low-income and low political participation, are rarely organised, so that their propaganda influence is weak. Art lovers should therefore not be afraid of the propaganda activity with referenda.

---

[60] Economic theory offers various mechanisms such as Clarke or Lindahl taxes to alleviate the problem that voters cannot express preference intensities. However, these methods require more information than is commonly available and none of these approaches can easily be incorporated in actual political processes.

- Judged by the size of historic conservation societies or by the number of visitors to art museums, it may seem that only a minuscule number of voters is prepared to support public investments in historic conservation programmes or the arts. This view is biased because non-use values represent a significant portion of the overall social value of preserving our cultural heritage. Many individuals value historic monuments and pieces of art but they never express this evaluation by visiting museums. In a referendum, these non-use values will be captured. For example, many citizens of Basle never visit the city's art museum and they have no intention of so doing. Nonetheless, these people frequently voted in favour of purchasing two Picasso paintings.[61] As an analysis of the Quebec museum has shown, the non-use values are at least as important as the use-values we commonly observe.[62] Therefore, the arts probably have many hidden supporters who we will only detect in budget or project referenda.

- Anomalies of choice will likely bias voting decisions in favour of historical conservation. The most important effect in this respect is the endowment effect.[63] Due to this effect, individuals asymmetrically weigh losses and gains. To lose an object one possesses is judged to be worse than to gain the same object. Imagine France losing the Mona Lisa, Rome the Colosseum, or the Uffici being destroyed. It is safe to predict that individuals would value such losses highly and be prepared to make considerable sacrifices to prevent losing them. Now, imagine a situation where none of these historic treasures was ever in the possession of these countries. Does Rome really need the Colosseum? (It has the whole Forum Romanum with its spectacular arches of triumph.) Does the Louvre really need the Mona Lisa? (It has hundreds of other masterpieces.) If

---

[61] B. S. Frey and W. W. Pommerehne, *op. cit.*, Ch. 10.

[62] F. Martin, 'Determining the Size of Museum Subsidies', *Journal of Cultural Economics*, Vol. 18, 1994, pp. 255-70.

[63] D. Kahneman and A. Tversky, 'Intuitive predictions: Biases and corrective procedures', in S. Makridakis and S.C. Wheelwright (eds.), 'Forecasting, TIMS', *Studies in Management Science*, Vol. 12, 1979, pp. 313-27; J. L. Knetsch, 'The Endowment Effect and Evidence of Nonreversible Indifference Curves', *American Economic Review*, Vol. 79, 1989, pp. 263-91.

endowment effects are present, people would have a very low willingness-to-pay to acquire yet another masterpiece, yet another Roman monument. Comparing the valuation of monuments over time, it is possible to observe the endowment effect at work. We mention just two examples: both the Eiffel Tower in Paris and the Rotunda in central Birmingham were not liked at all at the time of their construction. Today, few people can imagine losing these landmarks. By definition, historic preservation programmes are designed to restore and preserve what we already possess. Thus, the endowment effect works in favour of old buildings and historic monuments.

6. Conclusions

In view of tighter budget constraints and past public controversies, administrators have turned to cost-benefit analysis as a framework to evaluate and select historic conservation programmes. These analyses are valuable because they enumerate the gains and losses to society and allow the analyst to rank different projects according to their net present value. However, the methods that are currently used to measure the benefits of art institutions and historic conservation efforts are not without considerable flaws and require many, and sometimes quite arbitrary, assumptions. We have argued that, as a result of these deficiencies, public administrations will tend to 'err on the safe side', the safe side in this case being an overprovision of the public good which is in the interest of the public administrators and their relevant reference group, the arts community.

In our view, this bias can be corrected by reforming the political institutions. Citizens should be granted the right to vote on historic preservation budgets and major art projects. As we have pointed out, these new institutions will most likely not lead to a large number of popular votes because the public administrators take the threat of a possible referendum into account when preparing the budget. However, these institutions will lead to historic preservation programmes which conform better to the preferences of the median voter.

While this constitutional approach effectively solves the principal-agent problem, it may lead to an underprovision of art subsidies and historic conservation. This outcome is likely because the minority of art-lovers cannot express their intensive preferences at the polls. We have identified four effects which tend to decrease this underprovision of the public good and bias referendum outcomes in favour of the arts and historic conservation: voter turnout, information effects, non-use values and the endowment effect all lead to larger public budgets than the median-voter outcome implies.

The rôle of cost-benefit analysts need not be diminished under the proposed new set of political institutions. On the contrary, public administrators and politicians will find themselves under much greater pressure to justify the expenditures for the arts and for historic preservation when referenda are permitted. To the extent that cost-benefit analysis provides a rational framework to assess the social value of these investments, the demand for such analyses might even increase. Of course, the resources spent on communicating the rationale for historic preservation to the general public comes at an (additional) opportunity cost. However, public discourse might not only lead to decisions that conform better to the median voter's preferences, but there may be an additional benefit as well. It is well known that the enjoyment of the arts and of good architecture depends on the size of the relevant human capital. The more individuals know about the arts, the higher are the benefits they derive from the existing stock of cultural objects. The proposed political institutions thus lead to more democratic conservation programmes and they provide the public with additional incentives to learn about the arts by granting them the right to decide on budgets and large projects.

3

HERITAGE REGULATION:
A POLITICAL ECONOMY APPROACH

Ilde Rizzo*

University of Catania

1. Introduction

IN WESTERN COUNTRIES HERITAGE, buildings as well as works of art, is characterised by a mix of public and private ownership combined with government control. The relative weight of public and private ownership varies across countries as does the intensity and the range of government control. This paper aims to analyse the rôle that regulation plays in heritage, and which forms it takes, in order to attempt to ascertain whether it is regulation itself, its range and/or its intensity which affect the above-mentioned public-private mix.

Section 2 briefly reviews the main arguments put forward in the literature to provide a rationale for regulation in heritage. In Section 3, using a political economy approach, the theoretical arguments will be applied to comment upon the main forms that regulation takes, in an attempt to outline what are the peculiar features of regulation when applied to heritage and what policy implications can be drawn. In Section 4 some tentative conclusions will be offered.

2. Regulation in Heritage

As is well known, from the economist's point of view, the most widely accepted government approach to the cultural sector recognises that art activities are socially relevant, that markets are imperfect and need to be corrected to accord with individuals'

---

* I am grateful to Emilio Giardina, Isidoro Mazza and Giacomo Pignatoro for helpful discussions, useful suggestions and critical comments. Errors remain my responsibility.

preferences.[1] This approach provides a widely used framework for studying public policies in the heritage sector. Following this conventional normative approach based on 'market failure', and according to the prescriptions of welfare economics, a long-sighted government, adopting a 'public interest' stance, is assumed to provide efficient remedies for market failure, through the use of the different tools of government intervention.

As far as efficiency is concerned, the well-known arguments developed in the literature of option demand,[2] bequest demand,[3] national prestige,[4] public goods[5] and externalities[6] are usually put forward to justify public intervention in order to avoid under-provision of heritage services. Moreover, as Throsby stresses,[7] the

---

[1]   Another approach is to provide support for the arts, considered as a 'merit' good. This argument is controversial. On the one hand, it is argued that it shows a 'paternalistic' philosophy which is difficult to justify on rational grounds; on the other hand, it might be argued that adopting a concept of multiple individual preferences the contrast between merit goods and the consumer's sovereignty becomes an open question. According to Musgrave (R.A. Musgrave, 'Merit Goods', *Palgrave's Dictionary of Economics*, London: Macmillan, 1987, pp. 452-53), the conservation of art and culture may be considered a merit good in the sense that the consumer's sovereignty is substituted by another rule: individuals support and finance culture because they accept the 'community preference', even though their personal preferences may diverge.

[2]   'Option demand' refers to the individual's desire on his or her own or others' behalf of maintaining the option of gaining benefits from heritage in the future.

[3]   'Bequest demand' refers to the individual's desire to allow future generations to enjoy heritage benefits in the future (on the assumption that future generations will have the same tastes and technological possibilities as the present generation).

[4]   The argument assumes that countries gain prestige according to, among other things, their artistic heritage and would suggest that public intervention should be addressed to support the artistic works and buildings which attract external attention. The argument holds at any level of government – national, regional or local.

[5]   As is well known, the argument assumes that heritage exhibits two features – indivisibility and non-excludability: an extreme example is given by the fact that nobody can be excluded from the enjoyment of admiring the exterior of a building and that individual enjoyment does not preclude other people from doing the same. Congestion and the possibility of exclusion in some cases may arise.

[6]   The educational value of heritage as well as its effect on taste formation are usually taken into account.

[7]   D. Throsby, 'The Production and Consumption of the Arts: A View of Cultural Economics', *Journal of Economic Literature*, Vol. 32, 1994, pp. 1-29.

normative case for public intervention might rest also on arguments which are outside the conventional assumption of well-informed individuals underlying welfare economics. For example, in the arts individuals may be ignorant:[8] as a consequence, they might take decisions which might be out of line with their own interests and public intervention might thus be called for.

The above-mentioned normative arguments are too well known to require further attention here:[9] what it is important to stress is that, on these grounds, government policies are called for. Different mixes of government policy instruments – public expenditure, taxation and regulation – can be adopted according to prevailing economic and institutional settings. In the analysis which follows, attention will be concentrated on regulation: public expenditure and taxation will be recalled only to emphasise differences and/or analogies with regulation.

Regulation is a broad concept and various definitions can be provided. In this paper we refer to direct, non-monetary interventions by the government in economic activities.[10] This intervention is usually aimed at restricting or modifying the activities of firms and individuals in the private sector, within the framework of the policies pursued by government, using enforceable directives and involving penalties for non-compliance.

In the field under study, as Throsby states:

'regulation, in the sense of specific constraints or directives affecting behaviour, is possibly the most widely used tool in heritage

---

[8] Other aspects raised by Throsby, *ibid.*, refer to the fact that individual behaviour might be inconsistent because of misrepresentation, weakness of will or fluctuation of preferences and that cultural goods can be defined as 'irreducibly social goods' because they provide benefits which cannot be attributed to a single individual.

[9] See Throsby, *op.cit.*, and R. Towse, 'Achieving Public Policy Objectives in Arts and Heritage', in A. T. Peacock and I. Rizzo (eds.), *Cultural Economics and Cultural Policies*, Dordrecht: Kluwer, 1994, pp. 143-65.

[10] In other words, we confine our attention to the 'negative' component of regulation. Regulation has also a positive component: it is designed to expand the activity of particular sectors or to avoid its reduction; to fulfil such an objective grants, subsidies and loans are used. On this issue, see A. Peacock, M. Ricketts, J. Robinson, *The Regulation Game*, Oxford: Blackwell, 1984.

conservation, despite the fact that in most circumstances it is the instrument least favoured by economists'.[11]

Regulation to Control Stock of Heritage

The major object of regulation can be defined as the control of the stock of heritage, both buildings and works of art. The fulfilment of this objective is pursued by 'listing' the buildings as well as the historical and archaeological sites for preserving them, requiring the owners of buildings and of works of art to comply with the prescribed requirements. Within such a wide framework, just to provide some examples of the various means by which regulation can be implemented in heritage, we can distinguish regulation aimed at preventing the demolition of buildings, at imposing restrictions on the uses of the building, on appearance and on the way restoration and re-use are carried out, and at imposing limitations on the land use affecting heritage buildings.[12] At the same time, control over the export of works of art[13] is exerted to preserve the national stock.

Different links may exist among regulation and other forms of government intervention. Regulation may be used as an independent tool as well as a complement or substitute for other policies. In the first case, a 'classical' area is the definition of private property, both in the sense of protecting the rights of the creators of the works of art and in the sense of defining the limits of private property rights of heritage.

Regulation may be used as a complement to other policies whenever cultural private activities are publicly funded and asymmetric information problems, namely moral hazard, arise: for instance, if a private owner receives public financial support for restoration intervention, he will be compelled to carry it out according to precise rules and must allow admission of the public to the restored building.

[11] D. Throsby, 'Seven Questions in the Economics of Cultural Heritage', in M. Hutter and I. Rizzo (eds.), Economic Perspectives of Cultural Heritage, London: Macmillan, 1997.

[12] Throsby, 1997, op.cit., defines these forms of regulation as hard regulation to distinguish them from what he calls soft regulation – that is, non-enforceable directives (Charters, Codes of Practices, Guidelines, etc.) implemented by agreement and not involving penalties.

[13] On this issue, see below, Section 3, pp. 60ff.

Finally, regulation may be considered as a substitute for public funding whenever a public activity related to heritage is privatised. For instance, if a publicly owned building is sold to the private sector to be re-used, regulation can be used to ensure that government objectives are fulfilled.

As far as regulation in general is concerned, the 'public interest' theory based on the above-mentioned normative approach has been criticised mainly by questioning its normative content and the attention of economists has been directed to a closer consideration of collective decision-making processes.

It is assumed that regulators do not necessarily aim at pursuing the public interest and that regulated producers are not 'passive adjusters' to regulators, their relationship being depicted by the well-known 'principal-agent' paradigm. The way in which policy departs from an efficient outcome is complex and depends on various circumstances.

The most extreme interpretation of the regulator process has been provided by Stigler's well-known 'capture theory',[14] according to which regulation benefits the regulated. More realistically, it may be argued that the distribution of the benefits created by the regulation will depend upon the organisation costs faced by opposing groups.[15] If all the interests affected by regulation are equally represented, a relatively efficient outcome might result.[16]

Moreover, within a positive approach, it is important to distinguish actual from formal regulation. In practice, many regulations are not applied strictly: the unequal degree of application is reflected in the expected penalties and depends on the amount of resources allocated to discover and punish those who do not comply.[17]

---

[14] G. J. Stigler, 'The Theory of Economic Regulation', *Bell Journal of Economics and Management Science*, 1971, pp.3-21.

[15] S. Peltzman, 'Toward a More General Theory of Regulation', *Journal of Law and Economics*, 1976, pp.211-24.

[16] G. Becker, 'A Theory of Competition among Pressure Groups for Political Influence', *Quarterly Journal of Economics*, 1983, pp.371-400.

[17] B. Frey, 'Are there Natural Limits to the Growth of Government?', A. Peacock and F. Forte (eds.), *Public Expenditure and Government Growth*, Oxford: Blackwell, 1985, pp. 101-18. Frey provides a model in which endogenous limits to regulation are produced by the interaction between the government's intensity in regulation and the individual's compliance.

The positive approach to regulation provides interesting hints in the heritage field. It is worth noting that, because of the peculiar features of the issue under study, which will be explored further,[18] if 'capture' does exist it would seem to favour regulators more than the regulated. Moreover, the features of the decision-making process underlying regulation decisions are such that the chosen instruments – listing and the control of circulation of works of art – might not be able to fulfil the claimed government objectives in all situations. To develop such an argument, a closer analysis of what is meant by heritage regulation, with respect to both buildings and works of art, and of its policy implications, is required.

3. Heritage Regulation: Some Policy Implications

A peculiar feature of regulation in heritage is that the size of the regulated sector is not well defined *ex-ante* but is a matter of discretion of the regulator. In practice, unlike in most other cases, once the reasons for regulating are recognised, not only the choice of the instruments and their intensity but also the extent of regulation itself depend on the regulators.[19] Regulation, in fact, aims at controlling the stock of heritage, both works of arts and buildings: the identification of what is cultural heritage and, moreover, the process by which cultural heritage is identified are not unambiguous and deserve attention.

Even if different authors may provide different definitions of cultural heritage, it is widely agreed that heritage identifies a set of goods which belong to the past and are socially relevant because they are an expression of the cultural development of a society.[20] A good belongs to the set of cultural heritage if 'society' values it as a testimony to its cultural evolution and, as a consequence, the identification of cultural heritage should belong to some form of collective decision-making.

---

[18] See pp. 62-63 below.

[19] This is not the case in most sectors where regulation is applied. For instance, if government decides to regulate the electricity industry, the range of regulation is well defined.

[20] See C. Koboldt, 'Optimising the Use of Cultural Heritage', in M. Hutter and I. Rizzo (eds.), *op. cit.* In a wider perspective, heritage could be defined taking into account also the cultural value of modern artefacts as testimony of the present for future generations. Such a perspective becomes important when decisions have to be taken on the allocation of funds in conserving historical artefacts or in promoting new ideas.

Because of the information problems related to the artistic and historical features of heritage, specialists often play a central rôle in the process of identification of cultural heritage. Artefacts

'become identified as heritage goods usually by archaeologists and historians who have obtained some form of official recognition or public acceptance of their status as experts in determining their artistic or historical significance'.[21]

The institutional listing of cultural heritage existing in most countries, can indeed be considered as a solution to these informational problems and provides room for other actors, such as local councils, or government officials, to be involved in the process of identifying cultural heritage, even if they may not have any expertise at all.

As explained,[22] since there is no objective way of identifying what deserves conservation and what priority has to be established in setting the agenda for public intervention, the identity of those involved in this kind of decision is relevant in determining the size and the composition of the stock of cultural heritage as well as the significance of its elements. Even if it is difficult to relate the size of the stock of cultural heritage to specific influences, it should be noted that the identification of what is cultural heritage and, moreover, of what deserves to be protected vary through time[23] and that a growing range of conservation has been observed in some countries.[24]

---

[21] A. Peacock, *A Future for the Past: The Political Economy of Heritage*, Edinburgh: The David Hume Institute, 1994, p.8.

[22] G. Pignataro and I. Rizzo, 'The Political Economy of Rehabilitation: The Case of the Benedettini Monastery', in M. Hutter and I. Rizzo (eds.), *op. cit.*

[23] On this issue, see G. Guerzoni, 'Cultural Heritage and Preservation Policies: Notes on the History of the Italian Case', in M. Hutter and I. Rizzo (eds.), *op. cit.*

[24] F. Benhamou, with respect to France, points out two reasons for the extension of the objects included in the set of cultural heritage: 1) 'historical additions', since 'ever more recent buildings are included as they represent the national heritage of the future'; 2) 'typological extension', since 'new listings included gardens, original decor in restaurants, cafés, shops and swimming pools, parts of the nation's industrial heritage'. (F. Benhamou, 'Is Increased Public Spending for the Conservation of Historic Monuments Inevitable?', *Journal of Cultural Economics*, Vol. 20, 1996, pp.115-31.)

Additional Scope for Regulator in Heritage

A peculiar feature of regulation in heritage needs to be stressed: because of the impossibility of defining in an objective way the extent of regulation – what has to be regulated, how and therefore who is to be regulated – the regulator (the heritage authority) enjoys a greater range of freedom compared with those operating in other fields. The identity of the regulator depends on the institutional features of the regulatory decision-making process, which may vary among countries: in some countries independent agencies can be instituted while in others decisions are taken at the political level and implemented by bureaucracies. Broadly speaking, it might be assumed that the decisions regarding what should be regulated and its ranking are taken at political level on the grounds of expert judgements while decisions on how to regulate belong to those charged with implementing policies, usually bureaucracies. In most cases, as for instance in Italy, bureaucrats in heritage departments are themselves experts. Because both the range of regulation and the ways it is implemented are matters for discretion, it follows that the room for bargaining increases. Experts may favour styles in line with their school of thought and decisions will also be affected by the relative strengths of the different demands; as a consequence, in some circumstances, a conflict among the different objectives which can be pursued through different ways of carrying out conservation may arise. All in all, then, the inclusion or exclusion of certain artefacts from the set of cultural heritage, and the decision as to what type of conservation can be carried out and how, is the outcome of a complex game played by many actors.

Whether the 'capture' theory holds in this case is a matter for discussion. Though it is possible that the regulated may capture the regulatory process, for example in the regulation of land use affecting heritage buildings,[25] it seems that, for the reasons given above, regulators are more likely to 'capture' the regulatory process according with their own views and interests.[26]

---

[25] Zoning laws imposing restrictions on the economic activities (construction as well as other types of activities) which can be carried out are examples of regulation which can be influenced for private benefit because effective pressure groups are likely to exist.

[26] Moreover, in heritage regulation decisions seem to be less affected by the problem of asymmetrical information, which usually characterises other fields, and, therefore, there is less room for the regulated to 'capture' the process.

Among the various bargaining situations which can emerge, it is interesting to underline the potential conflict between different levels of government when heritage regulation power is assigned at central level and has relevant implications for urban policy carried out at local level. In this case, for instance, as usually happens in Italy, restrictions over building uses, appearance and the way restoration and re-use are carried out impinge upon the possibility of restoring and revitalising historical centres, usually one of the objectives in the political agenda of local authorities.

The strength of the restrictions imposed by regulation affects the mix of public/private ownership and has a bearing on conserving heritage and satisfying society's demand for conservation. If regulatory decisions are taken adopting a 'conservationist' stance, that is, if the list of buildings claimed to be of historical importance is enlarged and the preservation orders imply strict requirements, the investment and maintenance costs and also the costs connected with the restricted use[27] will be severely affected and, as a consequence, private investment could be discouraged.

Moreover, discretionary regulation may lead to a high degree of uncertainty. In fact, whenever, as often happens, heritage is the result of the addition of different styles and historical periods, any discovery which takes place during an intervention may reduce the space for planned uses.[28] The occurrence of such a situation depends on the extent of regulation and on the discretion in defining the ranking of what deserves to be conserved. When the extent is very large, as it is if a 'conservationist' stance is adopted, risk and uncertainty become too high to be borne by any private investor,[29]

---

[27] These costs may arise as a reduction in the benefits from conservation, for instance when there are restrictions on the alterations required to bring an old building up to the standards typical of modern buildings.

[28] This is, for instance, what usually happens in Italy where heritage authorities act according to the principle that calls for stopping any activity which is *perceived* as contrasting with the overall conservation of the site. The existing system of rules can be useful to explain such a situation: the heritage authority is liable for any damage heritage might suffer from the works carried out on the site, while no responsibility is borne for the economic damage caused to the owner, as a consequence of the fact that the planned use of heritage is interdicted.

[29] This issue has been explored by G. Pignataro and I. Rizzo, *op.cit.*, with respect to a specific case study.

and the size of private sector intervention is likely to be restricted, increasing the demand for public sector action. In such a situation, therefore, the only solution to the conservation problem is the public one and consequently the demand for public resources will increase.

Constraints on Resources

Severe constraints, however, are likely to arise as far as the availability of resources is concerned, especially in an era of budget stringency. The problem becomes particularly severe in countries, such as Italy, with a huge artistic endowment, dispersed all over the country,[30] where conservation, if extensive, imposes such high costs that these are not compatible with the size of public finances. The likely result might be that a highly 'conservationist' stance, which discourages private investment, may result in a very low level of conservation.[31] This can be the starting point of a vicious circle which, because of the strong, and unaffordable, pressure on public funds, produces further decay, further pressure on public funds, and so on.

Moreover, the costs imposed by heritage regulation on society include not only those borne directly by the regulated, and the public resources used to implement regulation, but also the indirect costs imposed on any activity which may interfere at large with heritage regulation.[32]

From the above arguments it follows that the process by which heritage decisions are taken is crucial: if it is driven only by specialists' interests it is likely to bring about consequences which will probably be in conflict with the claimed objectives of

---

[30] At central level, the Ministry of Heritage has recently defined the 'Heritage Risk Map': 57,000 items have been catalogued (almost 10 per cent of Italian heritage). According to such research, 51 per cent of Italian monuments are located in 6,470 small towns (that is, towns with fewer than 15,000 inhabitants).

[31] The same negative result is reached if private owners, because of the stringency of the prescriptions, undertake their activities without complying with the existing rules, the likelihood of such behaviour being greater the smaller the risk of punishment. When the extent and intensity of regulation are relevant, monitoring, in fact, cannot be exerted effectively because of the amount of resources required.

[32] A. Peacock (1994), *op.cit.*, refers to the considerable hidden costs involved in planning regulations requiring the diversion of roads to protect archeological sites.

regulation itself, leaving society's demand unsatisfied. The extent of such an argument depends upon the degree of autonomy experts are granted and, therefore, on the institutional features of the decision-making process.[33]

Analogous arguments can be put forward when examining regulation of the circulation of works of art.

The alleged rationale for regulating the circulation of works of art is the preservation of heritage, mainly aimed at the protection of future generations and national identity and prestige. Equity arguments might be suggested to improve the accessibility of these goods; in such a case the notion of accessibility which seems to be relevant is the geographical one.[34]

Some questions arise. The normative economic case for regulation rests on some strong as well as undemonstrated assumptions, namely that the *status quo* (that is, maintaining existing arts and heritage provision within domestic boundaries) ensures the fulfilment of the claimed objectives. As has been pointed out,[35] there seem to be no efficiency arguments for preventing the free circulation of works of art in all circumstances, and distinctions have to be drawn according to the identity (public or private) of the parties involved. Entering into the details of such a specific analysis is outside the general scope of this paper: here, the main conclusions reached elsewhere[36] will be reviewed, stressing that it is the conflict of interests between the domestic as opposed to the international community which seems to be the 'core' issue. Here a political economy approach offers some interesting insights.

In this case, the rationale for preventing the circulation of works of art outside domestic boundaries seems to be based on the fact that self-interested policy-makers might find stringent rules more convenient, their costs being borne only by the potential seller while

---

[33] See below, pp. 68-70.

[34] Regulation of the circulation of works of art only incidentally might affect social accessibility, because it is not exactly aimed at affecting taste-formation and education, while it is likely to be irrelevant for economic accessibility, because no effects are expected on the price of arts attendance.

[35] E.Giardina and I.Rizzo, 'Regulation in the Cultural Sector', in A. Peacock and I. Rizzo (eds.), *Cultural Economics and Cultural Policies*, Dordrecht: Kluwer, 1994, pp. 125-42.

[36] E. Giardina and I. Rizzo, *ibid.*

the benefits are spread over the whole population. Such a conclusion, which seems to contrast with the conventional wisdom, can be explained because those with stronger interests against regulation cannot be easily identified as an organised group: art collectors are not geographically concentrated and, apart from the common passion for art, they may have different interests when the details of regulation have to be decided.[37] With benefits scattered, the formation of an organised group is unlikely,[38] given that a public good problem arises. However, the issue of defending national prestige and identity is so appealing that politicians will support it, since they will be sure that the majority of citizens will sympathise with it, especially when protection is given to what is perceived as a 'national treasure'.[39]

Arguments for Regulating the Circulation of Art Works

When examining the rationale for the regulation of the circulation of work of art a distinction has to be drawn at least with respect to the private/public identity of the parties involved in the exchange.[40] When the exchange takes place between private parties, formal regulation may differ from actual regulation and the implications of an extremely extensive list need to be stressed. In practice, a protectionist stance may induce collectors and/or dealers to leave the official economy and to undertake their exchanges in the underground sector. The likelihood of such an event is greater the smaller the risk of punishment they face, which is a function of the resources government allocates to monitoring activities. The effectiveness of regulation is affected by the quantity and quality of

---

[37] For instance, should protectionism be extended up to 19th-century paintings or should it cover only old paintings up to the 18th-century? And what about the treatment of glassware, books, etc.? A small, effective interest group is less likely to be created in this case than in others, where well-identified producer groups are involved.

[38] A different conclusion may be reached where an important international art market exists and auction firms constitute a well-organised group. It might not be coincidental that Great Britain has the most liberal regulation of the export of works of art in Europe and, at the same time, the most developed art market.

[39] The regulation of the circulation of works of art in the EU may offer an interesting case study of such a positive approach. On this issue, see F. Forte, 'Towards a European Market for Arts and Culture Goods: Some Proposals', in M.Hutter and I.Rizzo (eds.), *op. cit.*

[40] Such an analysis is developed in Giardina and Rizzo, *op. cit.*

monitoring; when the object of monitoring is extremely wide-ranging, the unofficial market will inevitably increase. In practice, the range of application of regulation is *de facto* restricted; what it is important to emphasise is that the boundaries (defined through such a process) are not necessarily consistent with the rationale of government intervention in the cultural sector, being only the spontaneous result of the interaction between public policy and individuals.

Different arguments apply to regulations preventing the circulation of works of art when institutions (museums) are involved. In this case, the issue of accessibility provides a sound argument in favour of protectionism; in fact, under normal conditions (assuming that museums are not merely store-houses of works of art but places to which individuals have access) accessibility is likely to be reduced when a work of art is moved from a museum to a private collection. Moreover, under normal conditions, conservation, in the sense of preventing both deterioration and depletion of the works of art, is likely to be guaranteed by a museum at least as well as by a private collector and, therefore, also on these grounds the regulation of the circulation of works of art gains support. However, further qualifications are needed.

Recalling the analysis developed above (page ???), analogous arguments can be applied in the case of works of art. Also in this case, conservation imposes very high costs which are not considered affordable in countries particularly well-endowed with heritage artefacts. Again, from this point of view, the Italian case is extremely significant: in the period 1976-78 artistic endowments kept in public museums (at state, regional, provincial and communal level) decreased on average by 11·8 per cent, because of physical deterioration and depletion. In other words, keeping works of art within domestic boundaries does not ensure that national identity is preserved.[41] On the contrary, given the scarcity of available resources, relevant pieces may be severely damaged or may even disappear. As a result, the arguments put forward in favour of regulation become weaker even when museums are involved.

---

[41] G. Brosio and W. Santagata, *Rapporto sull'economia delle arti e dello spettacolo in Italia*, Edizioni della Fondazione Giovanni Agnelli, 1992.

In this latter case, however, precautions should be taken to prevent publicly-owned art stock from being compromised by unwise decisions, precautions of this kind not being required when the object of the transaction is private property. When public property is at stake the usual problems of the separation of ownership from control (with an extremely dispersed ownership) might arise, coupled with the absence of exchangeable residual claims.[42] In this light, the issue of controlling the managers and providing them with suitable incentives deserves attention and should precede any loosening of regulation.

From the above arguments it follows that the process by which heritage decisions are taken is crucial: if it is driven only by specialists' interests, aimed at acquiring recognition and stressing the relevance of the object of their study, it is likely to bring about consequences which contrast with the claimed normative objectives of regulation itself, leaving society's demand unsatisfied.

The Role of Society in Heritage Control

What rôle is society expected to play in this process? The issue is crucial and needs further investigation because of the following dilemma: while it is widely agreed that taxpayers have a legitimate claim to influence public decisions on this matter, it is at the same time true that specific knowledge and expertise are involved so that these decisions cannot be left entirely to taxpayers' choices. No clear-cut answers can be provided in this paper on this complex issue but some issues for further investigation will be raised.

First, it should be stressed that the process matters: forms of greater public participation in decision-making[43] as well as compulsory assessment, consultation or review procedures might be included in the regulatory process, though the benefits should be weighted by taking into account the likely increase in the

---

[42] When incentive arrangements based on exchangeable claims to the residual are ruled out, managerial performance closely depends upon the existing contractual possibilities and the costs of monitoring. On this issue, see M. Ricketts, *The Economics of Business Enterprise*, Brighton: Wheatsheaf Books, 1987.

[43] A. Peacock (1994), *op. cit.*, proposes that public participation could be enhanced if greater openness characterised the appointment of 'lay' persons to the decision-making bodies and if citizens who are active in heritage matters were allowed to vote for their own representatives within these bodies.

administrative costs and the slowing down of the process which would follow.

The problem we face – the need for a governance structure to define a mechanism available to society to restrain the discretionary scope of the regulator – is common to regulation in general. Of course, in the heritage field, for the reasons developed above, such a mechanism becomes crucial. In this respect, an interesting issue raised in another context[44] is that no unique solution can be provided to the regulatory governance structure, the choice being constrained by a country's institutional endowment[45] which affects the form and the severity of regulatory problems. Though it is not possible to devise specific proposals, interesting lines of thought can be derived in the sense that the improvement of efficiency and effectiveness of regulation requires further investigation as far as institutional features are concerned.

A further important issue is how the degree of public participation in heritage decision-making varies according to the distribution of responsibilities between different levels of government. The argument that devolution[46] increases the accountability of government is well known. In the heritage field the positive effects of devolution seem to be even stronger than is usually claimed because the links between regional/local communities and heritage are very close;[47] there is a vested interest at the decentralised level in the preservation and upkeep of heritage also for the beneficial

---

[44] B. Levy and P.T. Spiller (eds.), *Regulations, Institutions and Commitment*, Cambridge, Mass.: Cambridge University Press, 1996.

[45] B. Levy and P.T. Spiller, *ibid.*, identify five elements of a nation's institutional endowment: legislative and executive institutions, judicial institutions, custom and other informal norms, the country's administrative capabilities, and the character of the contending social interests, including ideology.

[46] The term devolution implies a stronger concept of autonomy than the term decentralisation and, in fact, with respect to cultural policy in general, is used to refer to the movement of responsibility to a lower level of government so that such a level has complete autonomy as far as policy-making, financing, management and performance are concerned, decentralisation being limited to the last two responsibilities. (J.M. Schuster, 'Deconstructing a Tower of Babel: Privatisation, Decentralisation and Devolution as Ideas in Good Currency in Cultural Policy', *Voluntas*, Vol. 8, No. 3, 1997.)

[47] A hierarchy of buildings might be established in terms of the geographical distribution of benefits deriving from conservation, whether it is national, regional or local, in order to decide the appropriate level of decision-making.

external effects that such an intervention can exert on the local economy (via its positive effects on tourism). Moreover, since the identification of those who gain and those who lose from regulation (and their interaction) become easier, the members of the latter group may have more room for organising themselves, acting as watchdogs rather than being only passive adjusters to heritage authorities' decisions. Additionally, in a more general perspective, it should not be forgotten that devolution would allow the possibility of using direct democracy tools, such as referenda, to assess public evaluation of heritage policies.[48]

4. Conclusions

The central argument of this paper is that in heritage – buildings as well as works of art – the extent of regulation and its intensity may be more conveniently explained using positive rather than normative arguments. The alleged normative rationale of the regulation of cultural heritage has been discussed and the pros and cons of regulation have been contrasted. The question 'whether, indeed, regulation is a suitable means to pursue government objectives' has been raised. No clear-cut answers have been provided but a general argument emerges: the range and intensity of regulation cannot be justified in all cases on normative grounds but distinctions have to be drawn according to circumstances since they often appear to be more the endogenous product of the public decision-making process than the appropriate tool to fulfil the claimed objectives of government intervention in the heritage field.

Shifting attention to the positive side, what seems to emerge is that the 'capture' theory does not necessarily apply in the heritage field and, if 'capture' does exist, it would seem to favour the regulators more than the regulated. The argument needs, of course, further investigation. Moreover, as a general conclusion, the idea that different rules affect institutions' behaviour and their accountability and responsiveness to the public gets further support, with the relevant implication that, when approaching the regulation of heritage issue, severe resource constraints must be taken into

---

[48] Swiss referenda offer interesting evidence on public attitudes towards the arts. B. Frey, 'The Evaluation of Cultural Heritage: Some Critical Issues', in M.Hutter and I.Rizzo (eds.), *op. cit.*, examines the arguments for extending the use of such a method to cultural decisions. See also Chapter 2 by Frey and Oberholzer-Gee in this volume.

account. Otherwise, the likely result would be that a highly 'conservationist' stance may result in a very low degree of conservation. This can become the starting point of a vicious circle which, because of strong pressures on public funds, produces further decay, further pressure on public funds and leaves unmet the objective of controlling the stock of heritage.

References

Becker, G. (1983): 'A Theory of Competition among Pressure Groups for Political Influence', *Quarterly Journal of Economics*, pp.371-400.

Benhamou, F. (1996): 'Is Increased Public Spending for the Conservation of Historic Monuments Inevitable?', *Journal of Cultural Economics*, Vol. 20, pp.115-31.

Brosio, G., and Santagata, W. (1992): *Rapporto sull'economia delle arti e dello spettacolo in Italia,* Edizioni della Fondazione Giovanni Agnelli.

Forte, F. (1997): 'Towards a European Market for Arts and Culture Goods. Some Proposals', in M. Hutter and I. Rizzo (eds.), *Economic Perspectives of Cultural Heritage*, London: Macmillan.

Frey, B. (1997): 'The Evaluation of Cultural Heritage: Some Critical Issues', in M. Hutter and I. Rizzo (eds.), *Economic Perspectives of Cultural Heritage*, London: Macmillan.

Frey, B. (1985): 'Are there Natural Limits to the Growth of Government?', in A. Peacock and F. Forte (eds.), *Public Expenditure and Government Growth*, Oxford: Blackwell, pp. 101-18.

Guerzoni, G. (1997): 'Cultural Heritage and Preservation Policies: Notes on the History of the Italian Case', in M. Hutter and I. Rizzo (eds.), *Economic Perspectives of Cultural Heritage*, London: Macmillan.

Giardina, E., and Rizzo, I. (1994): 'Regulation in the Cultural Sector', in A. Peacock and I. Rizzo (eds.), *Cultural Economics and Cultural Policies*, Dordrecht: Kluwer, pp. 125-42.

Koboldt, C. (1997): 'Optimising the Use of Cultural Heritage', in M. Hutter and I. Rizzo (eds.), *Economic Perspectives of Cultural Heritage*, London: Macmillan.

Levy, B., and Spiller, P.T. (eds.) (1996): *Regulations, Institutions and Commitment*, Cambridge, Mass.: Cambridge University Press.

Musgrave, R.A. (1987): 'Merit Goods', *Palgrave's Dictionary of Economics*, London: Macmillan, pp. 452-53.

Peacock, A. (1991): 'Enter the Regulators', in C. Veljanovski (ed.), *Regulators and the Market*, London: Institute of Economic Affairs, pp.79-84.

Peacock, A. (1996): *A Future for the Past: The Political Economy of Heritage*, British Academy Keynes Lecture, in *Proceedings of the British Academy*, Oxford: Oxford University Press, 1996.

Peacock, A., Ricketts, M., and Robinson, J. (1984): *The Regulation Game*, Oxford: Blackwell.

Peltzman, S. (1976): 'Toward a More General Theory of Regulation', *Journal of Law and Economics*, pp.211-24.

Pignataro, G., and Rizzo, I. (1997): 'The Political Economy of Rehabilitation: The Case of the Benedettini Monastery', in M. Hutter and I. Rizzo (eds.), *Economic Perspectives of Cultural Heritage*, London: Macmillan.

Ricketts, M. (1987): *The Economics of Business Enterprise*, Brighton: Wheatsheaf Books.

Schuster, J.M. (1997): 'Deconstructing a Tower of Babel: Privatisation, Decentralisation and Devolution as Ideas in Good Currency in Cultural Policy', *Voluntas*, Vol. 8, No. 3.

Stigler, G. J. (1971): 'The Theory of Economic Regulation', *Bell Journal of Economics and Management Science*, pp.3-21.

Towse, R. (1994): 'Achieving Public Policy Objectives in Arts and Heritage', in A.T.Peacock and I.Rizzo (eds.), *Cultural Economics and Cultural Policies*, Dordrecht: Kluwer, pp. 143-65.

Throsby, D. (1994): 'The Production and Consumption of the Arts: A View of Cultural Economics', *Journal of Economic Literature*, Vol. 32, pp. 1-29.

Throsby, D. (1997): 'Seven Questions in the Economics of Cultural Heritage', in M. Hutter and I. Rizzo (eds.), *Economic Perspectives of Cultural Heritage*, Macmillan.

4

THE EVOLUTION OF HERITAGE POLICIES

Françoise Benhamou

Paris X University and Laboratoire d'Économie Sociale

DESPITE THEIR NATURAL DIFFERENCES, historical buildings and artefacts are submitted, in France, to very similar regulations and laws. The economic logic is identical: the market is regulated in order to protect the historic or artistic interest of national heritage; buildings should be protected from alterations that would not match their historical and artistic characteristics, and artefacts should be protected against the threat of export.

These regulations are now applied in an ambiguous context: the concept of heritage is becoming more and more extended (Chastel, 1986; Choay, 1992), with the development of questions about memory and nation; and the increase in the number of protected monuments or artefacts is dramatic. At the same time, financial means are becoming scarce. Many analyses of heritage policies try to offer solutions to this contradiction by rationalising management, merchandising or sponsorship. But regulators themselves organise the growth of heritage under protection.

These regulations are generally analysed as resulting from the public characteristics of heritage goods (Peacock, 1976; Mossetto, 1992), because of :

- the indivisibility of the goods;

- their external effects, in the form of national pride, prestige, accumulation of human capital, tourism and legacy to be passed on to future generations;

- their option value, defined by what the non-user is prepared to pay to preserve the possibility of future utilisation.

Public authorities exercise an important power (Section 1 below), since they are in charge of the definition and production of heritage. The total amount of heritage increases with time, because public collections cannot be alienated, and this inalienability affects private collections under protected status (Section 2). The costs resulting from this increase imply the need to share the financial burden of restoration and upkeep between the state (or public institutions) and private owners. Our hypothesis is that this division is based on the limitation of property rights as a consequence of the regulations. From this point of view, regulations appear as the result of a balance of power between the state and the private forces of the market (Section 3).

This paper deals mainly with the French case, but reference is made to British policies. The proximity of regulations, despite national differences, inclines us to think that the problems are very similar in both countries, and more generally, in all countries facing conservation of heritage.

1. The Protection of Heritage

The official willingness to protect historic monuments from devastation and to protect works of art from being exported was asserted when the French Revolution began to organise the protection of chateaux and houses and to assert the importance for the Louvre to acquire important pieces that could otherwise leave France.[1] The first laws were passed at the end of the 19th century (in 1887), as in other European countries,[2] and changed in 1913.

The Laws

The law of 31 December 1913, which is still in force, provides, as in England,[3] for two levels of preservation:

- *listing* of buildings or parts of buildings 'of which preservation is in the national interest from an historical or artistic point of view';

---

[1] At the same time the French armies organised the plundering of Belgium and Holland, sending experts with their soldiers, who were charged with discovering and bringing back to France works of art which deserved to be kept in 'the country of liberty'.

[2] In England a law concerning ancient monuments was passed in 1882. In 1895 the National Trust was founded by a few owners. Its importance was recognised in 1907, when Parliament made its properties inalienable. Laws currently in force were adopted in 1953. In Italy important legislative decisions were adopted between 1902 and 1939.

[3] In England, too, regulations distinguish between scheduled and listed monuments (which are divided into three categories).

- *registration* in an additional inventory of historic monuments of 'publicly or privately-owned buildings or parts thereof which do not justify immediate listing but which are of sufficient historic or artistic interest to render preservation desirable'.

The law stipulates the protection of surrounding buildings (within a perimeter of 500 metres). The same law protects artefacts 'of which preservation is in the national interest from a historical, artistic, scientific or technical point of view'. Listing implies the prohibition of export and the obligation to be authorised every time restoration or repair is proposed.

In 1941, another important law was passed prohibiting the export of works of art that were not listed but for which preservation from export was in the national interest from 'an historical or artistic point of view'. Works of art above a certain value had to be declared. They were kept in storage for a few days and French curators had to decide whether the artefact should stay in France. If so, they could buy it for national museums, at the declared price ('retention right'). The aim of this law was to limit the export of works of art, to make public collection richer, *and* to penalise underrated declarations.

In 1993, with the abolition of borders within the European Community, this law had to be replaced by another regulation, the law of 31 December 1992, which distinguishes between three categories of goods:

- Works of art that can be freely exported.

- Works of art whose value exceeds a certain amount that varies with age (50 years) or the type of good (in 1996, 150,000 ecus for paintings, 15,000 ecus for drawings, 50,000 ecus for sculptures, but zero ecus for manuscripts and archives which can have an important heritage value and a less important market value). The exporter has to apply for an export certificate indicating that the work of art is not a   national treasure. If granted, this certificate is valid for five years. If refused, the work cannot be exported. The government has three years to decide whether or not to buy it, list it, or let it leave France.

- Listed works, and pieces of national collections, that cannot leave France.

Licences are granted or refused by *ad hoc* committees. The law, which is still in force, is compatible with the Treaty of Rome (Article 36) which recognises the possibility of excluding from free trade cultural goods that have the characteristics of national treasures. Members of the European Union control the definition of these goods. In Germany, for instance, each *Land* draws up a list of such treasures. In Great Britain, art trade was free until 1939. The war prompted the government to limit exports. In 1950, the Waverley Commission recommended checks on exports of important works of art.[4] A committee of experts decides in each case and collectors whose works cannot be exported are entitled to compensation.

An Interpretation of Heritage Laws

The definition of heritage is wide, including historical or artistic criteria. Therefore the responsibility to define national heritage, even in the case of private property, is left with public authorities and selected experts. As Alan Peacock notes (1994, p. 8):

> 'A large proportion of artefacts are not produced with the idea of reminding us our past, although there are important exceptions in the case of public buildings or memorials, particularly war memorials. They become identified as heritage goods usually by archeologists and historians who have obtained some form of official recognition or public acceptance of their status as experts in determining their artistic or historical significance.'

Heritage is *a posteriori* defined by experts who are given a large amount of leeway. Asymmetric information between experts and the public leads experts into the permanent temptation to apply scientific, aesthetic, or even personal considerations when they have to take a decision, instead of considerations about the public's needs or wishes, though taxpayers should have the possibility to express their own view. This is a classical problem of agency that emerges when an agent has more information than the principal.

'Historical or artistic interest', as French laws stipulate, thus constitutes a very broad conception of national heritage. In 1981, a Chinese jar from the yuan period was listed and could not be

---

[4] Defined on the basis of three criteria, concerning the historical link and artistic importance of the work of art for the nation.

exported (see page 86). In 1990, Mr Amon, who possessed a painting by Ingres, imported to France in 1953 and listed a few years later, tried to proceed against the cultural administration, but lost his appeal to the *Conseil d'État*: he wanted the painting to be sold on the international market, and considered listing as evidence of an abuse by the government. Both cases show that the French administration considers non-French works of art or imported works as parts of French heritage. Nevertheless, the field of non-exportable works has been limited for very recently imported pieces.[5]

The conception of heritage that prevails for monuments is very large too, as in Great Britain where Lord Charteris, the first President of the National Heritage Memorial Fund, created in 1980, declared what he meant by heritage: 'everything you want' (Hewison, 1994). Listed heritage in France involves recent monuments (such as villas built by Mallet Stevens or Le Corbusier), and buildings that constitute testimonies of the past: restaurants, gardens, factories, and so on. This widening concept leads to an ever-growing number of protected elements. As Pierre Nora (1994) notices, 'commemoration value' is ever more decisive among the criteria applied by the heritage administration.

2. The Increasing Amount of Protected Heritage

Once a building is listed or registered, nothing can lead to its removal, except a decree of the *Conseil d'État*. This happened once with the delisting of a building in Versailles in 1990, whose state of repair and artistic interest did not justify continued protection.

Public collections are inalienable. This status is inherited from the inalienability of the Crown's patrimony, but there are very few legal texts that specify which artefacts or collections are concerned (Chatelain, 1987): the only texts deal with libraries, collections of the Modern Art Museum, and a well-known decision of the *Cour de Cassation* concerning a painting which a collector wished to recover but which had entered national collections.[6] Inalienability implies the impossibility of sale and imprescriptibility: an object of a

---

[5] Heli de Talleyrand affair (1969), and Elido World Corporation affair (1977): the *Conseil d'État* recognised that the 1941 law could not be applied to very recently imported works of art, even if created by French artists.

[6] Montagne versus Réunion des Musées nationaux, *Cour de Cassation*, 1963.

national collection remains the state's property, even if it has not been displayed for many years.

Banning of export constitutes a derived form of inalienability, because it limits the right to sell, by maintaining the artefact in the country, and organising, as we shall see, the possibility for national museums to buy the object. And, once it is listed, it remains so for ever.

Requests to authorise export have nevertheless significantly increased since 1980 (Table 1). This increase is evidence that sellers wish to sell on the international market, where prices are much more attractive. In 1993 and 1994, after the new law came into force, 5,679 certificates were granted, and 21 refused. The question of what happens to works of art whose certificate is not given during three years is crucial : how could museums buy them after three years if funds remain unchanged? It was suggested that a part of the lottery's gains could be allocated to finance such acquisitions (Chandernagor, 1994). But this proposal only constitutes a transfer of the burden. The second proposal, de-accessioning, implies forgetting about inalienability, but would diminish the loss of income, for the museums, resulting from the market value of minor works that never leave stock storage and that could easily be sold.

Table 1: Requests for Export Licences, 1980-89

Year	Number of Requests
1980	5,600
1985	9,300
1989	11,000

Source : Direction des Musées de France, 1992. Each request concerns some 10 artefacts.

For example, at the Museum of Modern Art in Paris, only 5 to 10 per cent of the works are displayed, while a thousand works are bought each year: if display areas are not extended, the ratio of displayed works to works in storage will decline. Thus inalienability implies an ever-growing number of protected works kept by museums.

In the same way, we can observe constant growth in the number of monuments to be protected. The rhythm of entries of monuments
[continued on page 83]

Table 2: Number of Historic Monuments Listed: France, 1836–95

Period	1836-39	1840-49	1850-59	1860-69	1870-79	1880-89	1890-99	1900-09	1910-19
Number of Historic Monuments Listed	10	725	36	564	162	595	196	1,030	1,450
Cumulative Total	10	735	771	1,335	1,497	2,092	2,288	3,318	4,768

Period (cont.)	1920-29	1930-39	1940-49	1950-59	1960-69	1970-79	1980-89	1990-95
Number of Historic Monuments Listed	1,866	1,046	908	522	777	1,102	2,404	1,087
Cumulative Total	6,634	7,680	8,588	9,110	9,887	10,989	13,393	14,480

Sources: Agnus et Zadora, 1987; Ministère de la Culture, 1997.

Table 3: Number of Registrations in the Additional Inventory of Historic Monuments in France since 1970

Year	1970	1971	1972	1973	1974	1975	1976	1977	1978
No. of Registrations	188	381	350	353	480	631	278	456	321
Cumulative Total	16,546	16,927	17,277	17,627	17,980	18,460	19,091	19,369	19,825

Year	1979	1980	1981	1982	1983	1984	1985	1986	1987
No. of Registrations	321	322	270	268	235	850	268	739	795
Cumulative Total	20,146	20,467	20,737	21,005	21,240	22,090	22,358	23,097	23,890

Year	1988	1989	1990	1991	1992	1993	1994	1995
No. of Registrations	836	613	740	716	762	652	600	622
Cumulative Total	24,726	25,341	26,081	26,797	27,559	28,211	28,811	29,449

Sources: Agnus et Zadora, 1987; Ministère de la Culture, 1997.

into the 'list' is correlated with legislative changes (1887, 1905: separation of Church and State; 1913, 1984-85: decentralisation of registration). By the end of 1995 a total of some 44,000 monuments (Tables 2 and 3) and 200,000 artefacts were protected (see Table 4 which shows only 'listed' artefacts: it excludes those 'registered'). This count does not include the works of art kept by museums whose number may not be known even by curators (Grampp, 1989, Peacock, 1994).[7] Today some 47 per cent of the monuments and buildings listed belong to private owners. This growth generates congestion and leads to proposals to rationalise the management of monuments open to the public (Agnus, 1985). It is rarely seen as the result of the policy that organises the definition and production of heritage.

Table 4: Total Number of Listed Artefacts: France, 1983-94

Year	1983	1984	1985	1986
Total No. Listed Artefacts	111,202	116,431	117,512	118,520

Year	1987	1988	1989	1990
Total No. Listed Artefacts	119,807	120,607	121,137	122,437

Year	1991	1992	1993	1994
Total No. Listed Artefacts	125,937	127,545	128,376	129,559

Source: Ministère de la Culture, 1997.

---

[7] In the United Kingdom, scheduled monuments are less numerous, but those listed are far more numerous than in France, and are not automatically entitled to subsidies from the heritage administration.

Number of scheduled or registered monuments or buildings: United Kingdom, 1995

	Scheduled Monuments	Registered Buildings
Great Britain	15,443	443,000
Wales	2,830	12,256
Scotland	6,138	41,479

Source: Council of Europe, 1996.

3. Limitations on the Exercise of Private Ownership

Laws protecting monuments and laws protecting artefacts are inspired by the same doctrine: an object that is considered as an element of heritage generates (for its, possibly private, owner) duties and obligations that act as impediments to alteration, sale, or export. Laws indisputably restrict the sphere of personal freedom and of free trade.[8]

The Case of Historic Buildings

Private owners of listed monuments must meet a variety of obligations which are not negligible. When a building is listed as an historic monument:

- Its destruction cannot be decided without authorisation. The Architect of Historic Monuments, a civil servant belonging to the heritage administration, oversees the restoration work. He chooses the firms to be hired and asks for subsidies. He judges the quality of works when the owner has not gone through heritage administration to undertake restoration work; the administration can attack the owner if the expert judges that the work has not been carried out in accordance with the quality of the monument.

- The sale has to be notified to the Minister.

- The monuments have to be accessible to the public during 40 days per year for the owner to benefit from tax deductions (see infra).

- When the owner fails to repair the building (and when it needs urgent repair works), the administration can decide to execute the work and force the owner to pay 50 per cent of the expenses (law of 1966).

- Listing without the approval of the owner or expropriation are possible, when the building is threatened because of its poor state of repair (law of 1966).

---

[8] Guerzoni (1995) shows how Italian policies toward heritage have consisted in passing laws that restrict freedom.

- Alterations or building in the proximity of listed buildings requires official authorisation.

The *Fondation du Patrimoine*, recently founded by the Ministry of Culture on the model of the National Trust, has been endowed with prerogatives that constitute a limit to property rights. It can, in particular, expropriate owners in case of emergency.

Thus heritage policies are based on a legal transfer of authority and a limitation on the exercise of private property, but at a cost. The obligation to restore in conformity with artistic and historical characteristics implies additional costs for the upkeep of the building. The older the building and the more specialised the construction techniques, the larger the cost, because restoration implies both the hiring of skilled labour and the use of rare and hence expensive building materials (Bady, 1985; Leniaud, 1992; Benhamou, 1996).

At the same time, listing increases the market value of the building through compensation organised by the state:

- subsidies, that cover 20 to 40 per cent of the total amount; local subsidies can be added without any official limit;

- tax deductions for repair, management or caretaking fees;

- inheritance tax relief, if the building is open to the public.

These subsidies are generally justified as being compensation for the positive external effects of tourism created by historic monuments and the economic consequences of restoration work for the construction industry. Our hypothesis is that they constitute the response of the market to the limitation of property rights. On the other hand, many lawsuits are filed by neighbouring building owners who suffer from losses resulting, for example, from the prohibition on alterations of their buildings. They argue that the state exceeds its authority (Caron, 1989).

Limits to private property and compensation also exist in Great Britain: the local authority in charge of heritage can refuse or approve the demolition of or alteration to a protected building; in case of refusal, the owner can try to appeal against the decision. In case of rejection, he may request compensation if he can prove that the property cannot be rationally managed without alteration. He can require the local authority to buy the building. But if the building is threatened because of poor repairs, a forced sale may be imposed on the owner (Council of Europe, 1996).

Thus compensation has been progressively organised in Great Britain and in France under the pressure of owners. In this permanent sharing of the burden of heritage between public and private owners, laws and regulations reflect a balance of power.

A Predatory Government?

The 1913 law holds that the owner of a listed work of art can ask for compensation for the financial loss resulting from the impossibility of selling the work on the international market. But the law has not been applied. An example will illustrate this point. When, in 1981, the owner of a yuan jar decided to sell it, it was estimated at FF6.5 million. But, since he was forbidden to export the jar, he could obtain only FF2 million. He brought an action against the government, but lost and was not compensated. The *Conseil d'État* argued that the government had taken its decision 'in the general interest', a fact that 'excludes implicitly any compensation' (*Conseil d'État*, 7 October 1987).

For museums, forbidding an export became an easy way to buy works of art at the lowest price, their mission to enrich their collections being frequently confused with the mission of protecting heritage (de Saint Pulgent, 1994).

When a collector wishes to sell an important work of art, he tries to bargain for an authorisation to export. In 1989, the owner of a well-known painting by Picasso, *Les Noces de Pierrette*, wanted to sell it. The Minister of Culture negotiated a deal: if the collector was willing to buy another Picasso, *La Célestine* (price: FF100 million), and offer it to a national museum, he would be granted the authorisation to export. *La Célestine* can now be admired in the Musée Picasso, and *Les Noces de Pierrette* was auctioned to a foreign collector for FF315 million. The total number of goods affected by the export ban has not been great – one or two every year – but many purchases in the Customs (an average of 50 works per year) and bargainings have occurred during the same period.

The Walter case, in 1992, constitutes a radical change. Jacques Walter wanted to sell a painting by Van Gogh, *Le Jardin à Auvers*, inherited from his father. The painting was listed and estimated to be worth FF200 to FF300 million on the international market. It was

Table 5: Credits for the Acquisitions of the French National Museums, 1987-94
(millions of French Francs)

Year	1987	1988	1989	1990	1991	1992	1993	1994
Subsidies:	30·5	48·1	37·4	53·2	25·4	44·3	18·4	29·9
- *State*	*21·3*	*24·7*	*29·7*	*29·7*	*16·5*	*32·7*	*16·6*	*14·3*
- *Heritage Fund*	*9·0*	*23·4*	*7·7*	*22·9*	*8·4*	*11·0*	*1·5*	*15·0*
- *Other*	*0·2*	–	–	*0·6*	*0·5*	*0·6*	*0·3*	*0·6*
RMN*:	46·3	69·2	68·3	88·6	50·6	81·4	51·4	109·4
- *Revenues*	*42·5*	*40·4*	*49·2*	*47·7*	*46·4*	*57·6*	*40·6*	*77·3*
- *Gifts, Bequests*	*3·8*	*28·8*	*19·1*	*38·0*	*1·6*	*18·5*	*3·8*	*20·4*
Sponsorship	–	–	–	2·9	2·6	5·3	7·0	11·7
Total	76·8	117·3	105·7	141·8	76·0	125·7	69·8	139·3

* The Réunion des Musées Nationaux is the institution in charge of commercial activities for National Museums.

Source: Réunion des Musées Nationaux, 1997.

sold for FF55 million to a banker, Jean Marc Vernes. The previous owner filed a suit against the French government, which was ordered to pay FF145 million to Walter[9] – an amount larger than the total annual acquisitions budget (Table 5).

What happened that can justify this reversal? *First*, the economic environment has changed. The market is now an international one, where Paris no longer plays the most important rôle, and buyers of expensive pieces are often not Europeans (Table 6). Prohibiting export therefore constitutes a more important barrier. *Second*, the government used its power as an easy means to compensate for the weakness of its financial capacities. This judgement puts an end to the situation. Ironically, after the death of Vernes, *Le Jardin à Auvers* was again up for sale, but rumour said that the painting was not by Van Gogh. It was unsold at Drouot's, on 10 December 1996!

Table 6 : Sales figures of Christie's, Sotheby's, and Drouot, 1994
(in millions of dollars)

Christie's	Sotheby's	Drouot
1,138·18	1,198·18	618·18

Source : Journal des Arts, 1995.

In Britain, important works of art are not subject to inheritance taxes, as long as they are accessible to the public. In this way, collections can be held together. In the case of a sale, the seller has to pay the taxes except when the work is bought by a museum. If an export licence is refused, museums can buy the work (they have two to six months to decide); if they do not, the licence is generally granted. In order to help museums to buy expensive pieces, 20 per cent of the revenues of the National Lottery are dedicated to the acquisition or conservation of heritage (law of 1994). In Germany, the owner of a work of art that cannot be exported may request that it be removed from the list if 'circumstances have changed'. If this is refused and he can prove damage, he can ask for compensation. He also benefits from fiscal advantages (inheritance taxes, wealth taxes, adjustment taxes).

---

[9] FF422 million reduced to FF145 million on appeal of the judgement.

The Right Compensation

If regulations can be considered legitimate, the question is, then, how to fix the right compensation. Public economics, particularly environmental economics, has frequently to deal with this problem. Three questions emerge. *First*, who is concerned? *Second*, how important are losses and gains? *Third*, how can collective willingness to pay be evaluated?

Owners are directly concerned. In this case, a comparison between the market value of the work once listed, and the value of a similar work which is not, could constitute a good indication of the loss or gain of utility for the owner. But the problem gets blurred when we take into account the collective effects of protection. *First*, the admission price for buildings that can be visited or for the works displayed in a museum, does not provide a satisfactory indication of willingness to pay (Hendon, 1983; Greffe, 1990). *Second*, in this field where property rights are so frequently discussed, it is not easy to identify which agents are concerned with a decision (Lichfield, 1988; Benhamou, 1997). That is the reason why the history of regulations depends on the state of the market and the lobby of collectors or owners. One of the consequences of the protection of privately-owned historic monuments is that private owners can gain from the increased value of their property which has at least partly been supported by public funding. In Britain, on the other hand, the National Trust becomes the owner of the building, while the previous owner and two generations of descendants can continue to live there.

Jurisprudential activity indicates whether regulations correctly reflect the respective quantities of free trade and protectionism that the state of the market requires and what collectors and curators, whose interests are contradictory in the short term, are ready to admit.

Two cases show that laws are only compromises and unstable solutions between contradictory interests. If an export licence is refused for three years, the sale is stopped, but the owner is not compensated. In June 1993 a painting by a Swiss artist of the 18th century, Liotard, was auctioned for FF9 million, but the licence was not granted and the sale was frozen. In November 1995, '*Verre, bouteille de vin, paquet de tabac, journal*' by Picasso, could not find a buyer at Drouot's because it had been listed and could not therefore leave France. These examples show how regulations

89

weaken the market. But they do not change the sign of the trade balance, as Figure 1 and Table 7 show. Figure 1 shows that exports and imports move together, and the imbalance persists: France is a net exporter. As a consequence the question of the legitimacy of protection policies arises.

Great Britain, though less protectionist than France, suffers from a less important trade gap (Direction des Musées de France, 1996). Regulations can limit exports, but can hardly reverse the trends generated by the significance of the country on the international art market and by the importance of its heritage.

4. Concluding Remarks

Heritage policies suffer from three contradictions. *First*, restrictions on exports and the development of private collections are contradictory. If the circulation of goods out of national borders is restricted, collectors are likely to suffer a loss: regulations weaken the art market. Curators are in favour of such restrictions because they believe that they constitute a protection against 'excessive' exports. But, as Pierre Rosenberg (1994), the Director of the Louvre, asserts museums need private collections, which constitute stocks for future acquisitions, bequests and donations. Therefore museums need a strong market. For example, the increasing flood of exports of works of art (Figure 1), and the increasing gap between exports and imports, in February 1997 led French authorities to consider more severe restrictions on exports: export licences could be refused as many times as 'necessary', in order to stop exports without forcing museums to buy.

Second, heritage policies promote their own destruction by widening the definition of heritage. De-accessioning or delisting remain unthinkable for most European curators. But contradictions between rising costs and diminishing funds should lead to the opening of the debate (Montias, 1976; Peacock, 1994).

The *third* contradiction concerns long-term and short-term decisions. Heritage policies generally rest on the hypothesis that government knows best what should constitute our legacy to future generations. But reading the story of vandalism (Reau, 1994)[10] shows the propensity for the state to accumulate errors and to follow fashions or lobbies. Reau describes the different forms of vandalism

---

[10] Updated by Fleury and Leproux for the period 1958-94.

Figure 1: Exports and Imports of Paintings, France, 1980-1996
(in millions of French Francs)

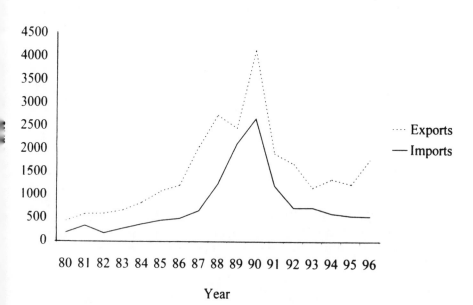

Source: Direction des Musées de France, 1996

Table 7: Imports and Exports of Works of Art: France, 1992
(in millions of French Francs)

	Exports	Imports
Paintings	1,684.9	725.2
Sculpture	174.6	36.1
Statuary	398.8	163.8
Other	702.9	337.7
Total	2,952.2	1,262.8

Source: Direction des Musées de France, 1996.

in France, distinguishing three periods: before 1789, during the Revolution and the Empire, during the modern period (1814-1914), and contemporary vandalism. He shows how the combined effect of real estate business, delays and bureaucratic procedures lead to accumulated errors and to the loss of many buildings that could have been saved:

> 'France adopted regulations a century ago, in order to protect its historic monuments, its architectural heritage, but every day serious prejudices are committed against this heritage. The complexity of regulations is partially responsible.'(Reau, 1994, p.1,028)

Criteria should be defined that take into account public welfare and create a coherent and logical list of priorities. The time a building is listed or registered depends entirely on an application made by private individuals, on the urgency of individual cases, or on the appreciation of the heritage administration. The result consists, as Ruskin (1850) suggested, in the French habit of leaving the buildings in a state of neglect, and restoring them much later. In the meantime, the collective costs of heritage continue to rise.

References

Agnus, J. M. (1985): *Economie du patrimoine: ressources économiques engendrées par le patrimoine monumental. Le cas du Mont Saint Michel*, Paris: Ministère de la Culture.

Agnus, J. M., and Zadora, E. (1987): *Repères sur les monuments historiques*, Paris: La Documentation française.

Bady, J. P. (1985): *Les monuments historiques en France*, Paris: Presses Universitaires de France.

Benhamou, F. (1996): 'Is Increased Public Spending for the Preservation of Historic Monuments Inevitable? The French Case', *Journal of Cultural Economics*, pp. 115-31.

Benhamou, F. (1997) 'Conserving Monuments in France : A Critique of Official Policies', in M. Hutter and I. Rizzo (eds.), *Economic Perspectives on Cultural Heritage*, London: Macmillan.

Caron, R. (1989): *L'État et la Culture*, Paris: Economica.

Chandernagor, A. (1994): *Les conditions du développement du marché de l'art en France: analyse et propositions,* Paris: La documentation française.

Chastel, A. (1986): 'La notion de patrimoine', in P. Nora (ed.), *Les lieux de mémoire,* Tome 2, Paris: Gallimard, pp. 405-50.

Chatelain, J. (1987): *Administration et gestion des musées*, Paris: La Documentation française.

Choay, F. (1992): *L'allégorie du patrimoine*, Paris: Le Seuil.

Council of Europe (1996): Comité du patrimoine culturel, *Rapport sur les politiques du patrimoine culturel en Europe: Royaume Uni,* Strasbourg.

Direction des musées de France (1996): *Étude sur les mouvements d'exportation et d'importation des biens culturels (1991-1992)*, Paris: Observatoire des mouvements internationaux d'oeuvres d'art.

Grampp, W. D. (1989): *Pricing the Priceless. Art, Artists and Economics,* New York: Basic Books, Inc.

Greffe, X. (1990): *La valeur économique du patrimoine*, Paris: Anthropos.

Guerzoni, G. (1995): 'Cultural Heritage and Preservation Policies: a Few Notes on the History of the Italian Case', paper presented at the 'Economic Perspectives of Cultural Heritage' Conference, Canizarro.

Hendon, W. S. (1983): 'Benefits and Costs of Historic Preservation', in W. S. Hendon, J. L. Shanahan, I. Th. H. Hilhorst and J. Van Straalen, *Economics and Historic Preservation*, Akron: Boekman Foundation, pp. 19-46.

Hewison, R. (1994): 'Retour à l'héritage, ou la gestion du passé à l'anglaise', *Le Débat*, Vol. 78, Jan-Feb., pp. 130-39.

Leniaud, J.M. (1992): *L'utopie française. Essai sur le patrimoine,* Paris: Mengès.

Lichfield, N. (1988): *Economics in Urban Conservation,* Cambridge: Cambridge University Press.

Ministère de la Culture (1991): *La politique culturelle de 1981 à 1991,* Paris.

Ministère de la Culture (1994): *Chiffres clés 1996,* Paris: La Documentation française.

Montias, J. M. (1976): 'Are Museums Betraying the Public's Trust?', in M. Blaug (ed.), *Economics of the Arts*, London: Martin Robertson, pp. 206-17.

Mossetto, G. (1992): 'A Cultural Good Called Venice', in R. Towse and Khakee (eds.), *Cultural Economics,* Berlin: Springer Verlag, pp. 247-56.

Nora, P. (1994): 'La loi de mémoire', *Le Débat*, Vol. 78, pp. 187-91.

Peacock, A. (1976): 'Welfare Economics and Public Subsidies to the Arts', in M. Blaug (ed.), *Economics of the Arts*, London: Martin Robertson, pp. 70-83.

Peacock, A. (1996): 'A Future for the Past : The Political Economy of Heritage', British Academy Keynes Lecture, in *Proceedings of the British Academy*, Oxford: Oxford University Press.

Réau, L. (1994): *Histoire du vandalisme,* Paris: Laffont (Bouquins).

Rosenberg, P. (1994): 'Les musées nationaux dans le marché de l'art', in E. Bonnefous, E. Peuchot, L. Richer, *Droit au musée. Droit des musées*, Dalloz, pp.59-74.

Ruskin, J. (1850): *The Seven Lamps of Architecture,* ???publisher and place

Saint Pulgent, M. de (1994): 'Sujétions et privilèges de l'État collectionneur', in E. Bonnefous, E. Peuchot, L. Richer, *Droit au musée. Droit des musées,* Dalloz, pp. 43-58.

5

THE NATIONAL TRUST: THE PRIVATE

PROVISION OF HERITAGE SERVICES

David Sawers*

Writer and Consultant

Introduction

THE NATIONAL TRUST is a remarkable organisation. It is the largest British charity and the largest English private landowner: owning 1·5 per cent of the land area of England, Wales and Northern Ireland, 164 historic houses, 19 castles and many other sites of historic interest and environmental value, it represents a sizeable part of the English heritage system. Its objectives, ever since it was incorporated in 1894, have been:

> 'promoting the permanent preservation for the benefit of the nation of lands and tenements (including buildings) of beauty or historic interest and as regards lands for the preservation (so far as practicable) of their natural aspect features and animal and plant life',[1]

to quote the National Trust Act of 1907, under which the Trust was re-incorporated.

The keys to the Trust's character lie in the words permanent, preservation and for the benefit of the nation. Most of the Trust's properties are inalienable, so that they cannot be sold. Nor can they be acquired compulsorily by the government, against the wishes of the Trust, without parliamentary procedures. The Trust was given

---

* The author is grateful to the National Trust for providing access to its archives; and to Mr Julian Prideaux, Ms Janette Harley and Ms Frances Garnham for their valuable assistance.

[1] *The National Trust Act, 1907*, London: The National Trust.

the power to declare its property inalienable by the 1907 Act, because it wished to preserve its share of the national heritage indefinitely. Its purpose was and is to preserve land and buildings for posterity.

These assets are preserved for the benefit of all the present and future inhabitants of England, Wales and Northern Ireland, not for the benefit of the members of the Trust. This concept of responsibility to the nation and to posterity, rather than to its members, has caused friction between the management and members of the Trust, especially in more recent years when its membership has grown large. Some members have felt that they share in the ownership of the Trust's property because they share in financing it; and they have also felt that members should be able to determine the Trust's policies. But the influence of the members of the Trust is limited, as is true in most English charities: the trustees – in the case of the National Trust, the members of its Council – exercise the ultimate control over policy, and the power of the Trust's members is limited to electing half the members of the Council, approving the Trust's accounts, and passing non-binding resolutions at the annual general meeting. Members can influence but not determine policy.

The Council considers itself responsible to the nation, not the membership, for the management of the Trust. There is a grey area, however, over the extent to which the Council should, and does, allow its policies to be influenced by the opinions of the membership. The Benson report on the Trust's constitution in 1968 suggested that members should be able to require the Council to examine an issue and report its decision to the members, if a resolution requesting this action was passed at AGM; but this suggestion was not implemented.

The unconditional nature of the Trust's obligation to preserve the property it acquires has proved a valuable asset. Much of the Trust's property has been donated: knowing that the property will be protected in perpetuity encourages owners to give the Trust properties they wish to see preserved. This knowledge has also encouraged governments to give the Trust financial assistance, in the form of grants or tax concessions additional to those any charity receives, which have aided its growth.

1. How the National Trust Has Evolved

The priorities of the National Trust have passed through four overlapping stages, according to David Cannadine.[2] In the first stage, from 1895 to 1920, its main concern was preserving open spaces and modest, mostly medieval buildings; in the second stage, from 1920 to 1949, it was concerned with promoting the 'spiritual values' associated with rural life; in the third stage, from 1935 to 1970, its main priority was protecting country houses and their contents from destruction or dispersal and with protecting the coast; and in the fourth stage, from 1965 to the present day, it has become more concerned with protecting the environment. Its membership has increased at an accelerating rate throughout its life: only 713 in 1920 and 6,800 in 1940, it reached 157,000 in 1965, 539,000 in 1975, one million in 1981, two million in 1990 and exceeded 2·5 million in 1997.

The founders of the Trust wanted to protect the beauty of the British landscape and its historic buildings from the effects of urbanisation, railway-building and tourism. Their priority was the acquisition of beautiful countryside rather than buildings – perhaps because the Trust then lacked the financial means to restore and maintain houses. When the Trust obtained its first country house in 1907, it lacked the funds to restore it. Its main acquisitions were land in the Lake District, financed by public appeals. At this stage in its existence, the Trust was small and relatively unimportant.

The 1920s saw the Trust gain in size and influence. Its members included Stanley Baldwin, Prime Minister from 1924 to 1929 and from 1935 to 1937, and other leading, mostly conservative, politicians. The cult of the countryside, as representing the best aspects of English life and the English character, was promoted by Baldwin and other members of the Trust such as the historian G.M.Trevelyan and the architect Clough Williams-Ellis. Trevelyan saw the Trust as a protector of the English countryside from the builder and the car. With such prominent supporters, the Trust was able to raise more money to buy more countryside and historic sites such as the land around Stonehenge, so that by 1940 it owned 68,000 acres. It was also given such historic buildings as Bodiam

---

[2] David Cannadine, 'The First Hundred Years', in Howard Newby (ed.), *The National Trust: The Next Hundred Years*, London: The National Trust, 1995.

Castle and Montacute House; but its priorities remained the acquisition of beautiful countryside or historic sites that might be threatened by development.

Changed Priorities: Country-House Scheme

The change in its priorities towards acquiring country houses which were in danger from demolition or the dispersal of their contents, began in the 1930s. Inheritance tax reached a top rate of 50 per cent in 1930, and the depression reduced landowners' incomes. The Marquess of Lothian, who had inherited four country houses in 1930 and been compelled to divest himself of two of them to help settle his tax bill, told the annual general meeting of the Trust in 1934 that the country houses of Britain represented a unique artistic treasure, which was under sentence of death from taxation. He urged that the Trust should concern itself with their preservation.

The Trust responded with its Country-House Scheme. Owners of country houses could give their house to the Trust, along with an endowment to produce the income needed to maintain it, and go on living in the house rent free so long as the public was admitted to see it. The Treasury also agreed that the owners would not be taxed on the value of their rent-free accommodation. This deal has been the basis on which the Trust has accumulated most of its present stock of country houses. The increase in the rate of inheritance tax to a maximum of 75 per cent in 1946, the high rates of income taxes and the rising real cost of labour all strengthened the incentive for owners to hand over their property to the Trust. This process was helped by the establishment of the National Land Fund in 1946 by Hugh Dalton, then Chancellor of the Exchequer and a supporter of the Trust – he made the Trust the main beneficiary of his own will. The purpose of the Fund was to compensate the Treasury for inheritance taxes forgone if property was given to the state in lieu of these taxes. The scope of the Fund was later extended to include the contents of houses and other artistic treasures and land given as an endowment was also exempted from inheritance tax; but only £19 million had been spent from the Fund before it was replaced by the National Heritage Memorial Fund in 1980.[3] The number of houses acquired by the Trust increased rapidly: 65 were obtained between 1940 and 1959, and 13 more in the 1960s.

---

[3] Jennifer Jenkins and Patrick James, *From Acorn to Oak Tree*, London: Macmillan,1994, p.138.

The size and character of the Trust were transformed by these acquisitions: it had gained its current repute as the custodian of country houses. The basis had now been laid for its rise to mass membership: visiting a country house became a normal way of spending a Saturday or Sunday, as incomes and car ownership increased. Membership of the National Trust was a convenient means of reducing the cost of such visits – members have free admission to its properties. Membership rose rapidly, as noted on page 97, so that by 1997 it had reached over 2·5 million.

The management of the Trust had to become larger and more professional to cope with this vast increase in its assets – and of assets of historical and artistic value, which required skilled maintenance if not restoration. It therefore gained a staff of land managers, conservationists, surveyors and art historians, who made an intermediate layer in the Trust's structure between the Council and the growing number of members. The direction of the Trust remained predominantly aristocratic: the Earl of Crawford and Balcarres was chairman from 1945 to 1965, and the Earl of Antrim was chairman from 1965 to 1977. The gap between members and Council was widening, and the Trust was gaining a managerial staff that was subject to professional peer pressures.

Professional Management and Sensitivity to the Environment: Operation Neptune

These changes helped to make the Trust more sensitive to the concern for the environment that developed in the 1960s. The emphasis of its acquisitions switched back from country houses to landscapes, and the maintenance of traditional forms of vegetation and wildlife on the Trust's land. Historic country houses were only accepted if they were among the best of their kind, if there was no other way of preserving them, and if they were generously endowed to cover maintenance costs: 13 were acquired in the 1970s, and 11 in the 1980s. The then Director-General of the Trust, Angus Stirling, wrote in 1985 that the National Trust adhered to the ideals of its founders, whose main concern was the preservation of unspoilt, beautiful countryside.[4]

The first big campaign to demonstrate the revised priorities was Operation Neptune, to protect by purchase the remaining unspoiled

---

[4] Sir Angus Stirling, Leading article, *The National Trust Magazine*, Midsummer 1985.

stretches of the coastline of England, Wales and Northern Ireland. This project made the Trust the owner of 565 miles of coastline by 1997; but it also led, in the short term, to conflict with some of the members, leading to changes in the constitution of the Trust.

The fund-raiser recruited to raise money for Operation Neptune, a grandson of one of the founders of the Trust, was dismissed after disagreements with the management. He retaliated by campaigning against the management, accusing it of being unrepresentative of its members' views, oligarchic, too deferential to the former owners of its country houses, and inefficient. The result was the appointment of an inquiry into the Trust's management, organisation and responsibilities. It was chaired by Sir Henry Benson, an accountant who was then widely employed as a trouble-shooter by government and industry.

He reported in 1968 that the Trust needed a more formal administration than it had had in the past, to suit its increased size. Nearly all his recommendations were accepted by the Trust, and they formed the basis for the Act of 1971 that describes the present constitution of the Trust. Since then there have been three more, smaller-scale inquiries into relations between members and management and into the management of the Trust. These inquiries have led to better methods of informing the Trust's many members about its activities, at national and local levels, and strengthened the position of the staff in relation to the committee members in the management of the Trust. Although the growing membership of the Trust has helped to provide a large increase in its income, the maintenance needed by its many houses absorbs most of its funds. In 1997 there was a backlog of maintenance amounting to £250 million. Acquisitions, largely of land, amounted to £7 million in 1996-97 and to £10·8 million in 1995-96 out of total expenditure of £141 million in 1996-97 and £149 million in 1995-96.

By 1996-97 the subscriptions of members supplied 29 per cent of the Trust's total income of £166 million, making them much the largest source of the Trust's income. As in other British charities, legacies are an important source of income, providing 16 per cent in 1996-97, while investments provided 14 per cent and rents 10·5 per cent. Admission charges to its properties produced only 5 per cent of its income. The Trust is unusual among British charities in obtaining so much of its income from its members; but it is, of course, also unusual in having so many members. The balance of its income comes from grants, gifts, special appeals, profits on its trading activities and other income and profits from its property.

The size of the Trust's membership is a social phenomenon. At the disinterested level of social concerns, it seems to reflect a widespread desire to contribute to the protection of the national cultural heritage and the natural environment; at the interested level of private profit, it reduces the cost of cultural days out in the countryside, visiting country houses. The Trust has benefited from the greater affluence, education, interest in the arts and the environment of the British people in a way that the state-financed artistic institutions have been unable to emulate. The annual subscription to the Trust may be only £27 and the average entry fee to a large house £4 to £6, but the Trust's experience shows that millions of people are prepared to pay these amounts to support, and benefit from, heritage activities.

2. The Present Constitution of the National Trust

The limited power of members is the aspect of the National Trust's constitution that has attracted most attention and attacks. As is legally required in British charities, the responsibility for running the Trust is vested in trustees – who, in the case of the Trust, are in effect the members of its Council. The details of the present constitution of the Trust are specified in the Act of 1971, which states that:

> 'The affairs of the National Trust shall be administered by a council
> ...consisting of 52 persons of whom 26 shall be elected members and
> 26 shall be appointed members', and that 'The entire business of the
> National Trust shall be arranged and managed by the Council ... and no
> regulation made or resolution passed by the National Trust in general
> meeting shall invalidate any prior act of the Council.'[5]

The Council also has the power to appoint the officers of the Trust and to determine their salaries. But the Council can, and does, delegate many of its responsibilities to an executive committee, whose members are appointed by the Council. The Council can permit the executive committee to exercise almost all its powers, except for certain basic policy issues that can only be determined by

---

[5] *The National Trust Act 1971*, London: The National Trust, paras.6(1) and 11(1).

the Council. The executive committee in turn has the power to appoint the members of regional committees and their chairmen.

Minor Role of Trust's Membership

There is thus little place for the members in the management of the National Trust: electing half the members of the Council, and proposing and voting on resolutions at the annual general meeting, are their most important powers. But the Act does state that resolutions passed by the members cannot override decisions of the Council; resolutions will therefore affect the Trust's policies only if the Council and committees are swayed by the members' arguments, or consider it politic to implement their opinions. Lord Oliver, in a report on the constitution commissioned by the Trust in 1991, argued that resolutions of a general meeting could not bind the Council because it had the status of the trustees of a charity, and the trustees are responsible for the operation of the Trust. He concluded:

> 'No resolution of the members can bind the Council in the performance of its fiduciary duty or enjoy anything higher than an advisory or admonitory status.'[6]

The Act, and Lord Oliver's interpretation of it, gives members rather less influence than had been proposed in the Benson report of 1968. Benson had suggested – though this proposal was not incorporated in the Act – that the constitution should give members the right to propose resolutions at the annual general meeting that asked the Council to examine a matter relevant to the Trust. If the resolution were passed, the Council should be required to undertake this examination, and to report its decision to the members – presumably at the next annual general meeting. However, Benson concluded:

> 'In making these proposals we wish to emphasise that the task of running the Trust must necessarily devolve on the Council. The members are entitled to make their views known and it is most unlikely that a view that clearly reflects the opinion of a majority of members will be disregarded. But the ultimate decisions of policy must be taken by the Council. If the members of the Trust feel that the Council is not

---

[6] *The Oliver Report on the Constitution,* London: The National Trust, 1993, p.18.

sufficiently receptive to their views, they will be able to propose at an annual general meeting the election of members of the Council in place of those retiring by rotation.'[7]

Members have proposed resolutions on aspects of the Trust's policy at many annual general meetings since the present constitution came into operation. But the effect of these resolutions on policy is difficult to establish: the Council often accepts the principle of a resolution, but it is then difficult to judge whether the Trust's behaviour has been changed to follow the proposed course. The small proportion of members voting for a resolution reduces their impact: normally only 5 per cent of members may support a resolution. The highest proportion recently voting was 7 per cent, on the issue of hunting, although 17 per cent voted in 1982, when the Trust's membership was smaller, and its management was attacked over its decision to lease land to the Ministry of Defence.

Little Influence over Council's Composition: Slow to Change

The right to elect half the members of the Council does not give the members of the Trust as much influence over the composition of the Council as Benson seems to have expected. Members have to judge the merits of the candidates on the strength of a 100-word note describing their experience, interests and objectives. Few members vote – in 1995, the largest number of votes for a candidate was 48,000, although more than 2 million members were eligible to vote – and they tend to support members of the Council standing for re-election. Changes in the membership of the Council therefore tend to come slowly.

The appointed members of the Council come from 26 organisations with interests that parallel those of the Trust. They were listed in the various acts that have determined the Trust's constitution, and the list can be amended by a vote of members at the annual general meeting every six years. These appointed members were intended to bring relevant expertise to the Council, not to act as representatives of the organisations from which they come.

The development of the Trust's management over the last 35 years has increased the influence of the staff over that of the

---

[7] *The Benson Report on the National Trust*, London: The National Trust, 1968, pp.35-36.

Council and committee members. This change was inevitable, as the size of the Trust increased; but it has reduced the opportunities for ' members to influence policy. Many decisions will be taken by the staff, on the basis of specialised knowledge that few members are likely to possess, and of information that will also be available to few outsiders. This growth in the importance of expertise has offset efforts to improve the supply of information to members about the Trust's work: they receive a 60-70-page magazine three times a year and a newsletter reporting events in their region. But there will be relatively few members who can provide informed comments on most aspects of the Trust's policies, whether they relate to the conservation of paintings in the Trust's houses or the management of ancient woodlands.

3. Interventions by Members in National Trust Policies

Members have shown the strongest interest in subjects that relate to political as well as to Trust policies. The two most contentious issues in the last 20 years have been the lease to the Ministry of Defence of land owned by the Trust at Bradenham, Buckinghamshire, to construct an underground control centre; and the hunting of deer and foxes on land owned by the Trust. The first issue led the Trust to improve its communications with its members, and to resolve that any application from a public authority to use inalienable land should be referred to the Council if there was any doubt about the decision. The second issue led to the appointment of Lord Oliver, a retired Law Lord, to review the constitution of the Trust and the rôle of its members; he concluded that they could only have a subsidiary rôle, because of the Trust's status as a charity (see Section 2 above). But there have also been a number of resolutions passed by annual general meetings which relate to issues more specific to the activities of the Trust, which may have had some influence on its policies. At the least, their passage has informed the Trust's management of the views of the more active members.

The dispute over the land at Bradenham showed that the Trust's committee members were politically naïve and out of touch with the opinions of many members. The Regional Committee considered that the request to lease inalienable woodland for use as a military installation did not need to be referred to the Trust's head office. When it was later referred, the Executive Committee and Council agreed to the lease because they believed that the Ministry of

Defence would invoke compulsory purchase procedures, which could overrule the Trust's protection of the land, if the Trust refused to grant a lease. (Land that has been declared inalienable by the Trust can be taken for public uses if certain conditions are met, but the case would be heard by a parliamentary committee or, if compulsory purchase is sought, at a public inquiry if the Trust refused to grant a lease.)

Once news of the lease reached members, the Trust's management learned that some members belonged to the Campaign for Nuclear Disarmament and other peace movements; and that they, and many other members, did not like to see inalienable Trust property used for military purposes. Opponents of the lease convened an extraordinary general meeting that was attended by 2,000 members, and although the management won the vote by 169,000 to 26,000 – about 17 per cent of members voted on this occasion – it realised that it had to improve its contacts with the members. The conflict could have been avoided if managers and committee members had understood the opinions of members better, and if they had thought it desirable to explain their decision to the membership.

Arkell Committee Suggests Basic Improvements

The result was the appointment of the Arkell Committee to advise on ways of improving relations between management and members. It suggested some basic improvements: members should be given more information, especially at regional level, and invited to comment; they should be more involved in selecting the members of regional committees; and the work of the Trust should be publicised more effectively. Probably the most important reform would be for the management to appreciate what could anger members, and act more circumspectly. The attitudes of managers needed changing, as Sir Angus Stirling appreciated when he became Director General in 1983. He found the staff of the Trust inward-looking, not sufficiently interested in external opinion, and not conscious of the Trust's rôle in the outside world.[8]

The present era for the National Trust can be dated from the Arkell report and Sir Angus Stirling's appointment as Director General. In the 14 years following 1983, there was one major

---

[8] Jenkins and James, *op.cit.*, p.303.

confrontation between management and some members, over hunting, which was not relevant to the main purpose of the Trust. But there were also several occasions when resolutions proposed at annual general meetings criticised the Trust's policies, or requested that new policies should be adopted. Seven of these resolutions were likely to have been referred to the Council for a report back to the members, if Benson's recommendation had been adopted, because they raised important issues. Their treatment therefore gives some idea of the extent to which the Council does follow the approach recommended by Benson.

Effects on NT Policies: Acquisitions

1. Acquisitions policy was the first and most important issue raised in a resolution from members. In the early 1980s the Trust had acquired several large country houses. This cluster of acquisitions was largely fortuitous, because the death of their owners, or changes in their plans, created the opportunity for the Trust to acquire most of these houses, and there was no other protector available for them. But some members believed that the Trust was giving a higher priority to acquiring country houses than to its other activities. These members therefore put forward a resolution at the annual general meeting in 1984, asking for a review of the Trust's policy on acquisitions. It suggested that the large number of recent acquisitions of houses might have reduced the Trust's ability to acquire sites of natural beauty, at a time when threats to the countryside were mounting. It urged the Council to re-assess its policies, and to give a higher priority to acquiring open spaces.

    The Council responded by supporting the resolution, and by assuring members that the recent acquisitions of houses did not prejudice the acquisition of open spaces. The Council's policy was to ensure that the Trust could acquire places of historic interest or natural beauty without either suffering at the expense of the other. (This statement was not as absurd as it may seem: the Trust acquired houses only if they were endowed with enough funds to cover their future maintenance, so that there should be no cost to the Trust.) At the meeting, a member of the Council explained that the Trust only sought to acquire open spaces, not historic houses. The best people to run a country house were the family that owned it; the Trust should act only as a safety net if the family could not retain a house. The Council agreed, however, that it would review the Trust's acquisitions policy.

The results of this review were published in the Trust's annual report for 1986. It emphasised the need for flexibility in the principles applied to acquisitions policy, because every property was different. But it repeated what had been said at the 1984 meeting: that the Trust regarded itself as a safety net for historic houses, so that it would only take over a house if all other means of preserving it had been found wanting, and if it was adequately endowed to cover its maintenance costs. The Trust would be failing in its duty, however, if it abandoned the protection of country houses. By contrast, the Trust would actively seek to acquire coast and open countryside.

The three main principles governing acquisition were:

'(a) The property must be of national importance because it is outstanding for its natural beauty or historic interest.

(b) There must be adequate benefit to the nation, including public access...

(c) Property will not normally be acquired for preservation unless the Trust is the most appropriate owner and, without the Trust's protection, it would be in danger of deterioration, demolition, alterations or development in a way that would be harmful to its character or environment.'[9]

The Trust's Council, in this instance, followed the procedure suggested in the Benson Report: it took a resolution from the membership, considered it, and reported back to the members (two years later) in the annual report. Policy does not seem to have been changed in the process, but the knowledge that some members were anxious to see more open country protected may have influenced some purchasing decisions. It may be significant that in 1990 the Director-General reported that no historic houses had been acquired for four years, until the acquisition of A La Ronde (itself a small house). The principles governing acquisitions leave so much discretion to the

---

[9] *Annual Report of the National Trust for 1986,* pp.6-7.

Executive Committee that it can buy almost anything: this degree of discretion may leave more scope for decisions to be influenced by the opinions of members, or the public.

Policy on Maintenance of Lake District Land

2. The second important issue raised in a resolution from members was the maintenance of the Lake District hillsides, walls and buildings. In 1984 and in 1986 resolutions were proposed by Dr John Wilks, drawing attention to the degradation of the topsoil on hillsides in the Lake District, caused by the many people walking over them. He urged the Trust to do more to alleviate the problem, and to improve maintenance of the stone walls and buildings the Trust owned. His resolution was passed in 1984, although the Director-General assured the meeting that the Trust appreciated the importance of the Lake District, and had launched an appeal in March 1984 to raise money for the maintenance of its Lake District properties. In 1986 his second resolution, expressing disappointment at the level of effort devoted to raising money for the Lake District fund and urging the Trust to raise an additional £1·5 million a year, was defeated after the Council proposed an alternative resolution endorsing its efforts to improve maintenance in the Lake District.

Dame Jennifer Jenkins, who was then chairman of the National Trust, has said of this episode:

'An institution never finds it easy to be pilloried, and Dr Wilks did not temper his criticism with emollience, but he undoubtedly performed a service in drawing attention to the needs of the Lake District.'[10]

It is also true, however, that the Trust had launched a special appeal to raise money for maintenance in the Lake District some months before Dr Wilks put forward his first resolution, urging more expenditure in the area. The implication of Dame Jennifer Jenkins's remarks is that the publicity created by Dr Wilks's resolutions helped the Trust to raise funds for this cause. But the Trust's policy does not seem to have been changed.

---

[10] Jenkins and James, *op. cit.*, p. 315.

Investment Policy

3. The third important issue raised at annual general meetings was
the investment policy of the Trust. A member asked at the 1987
meeting whether the Trust had considered investing in ethical
investment or unit trusts. The reply was that the Trust's funds
were managed by Robert Fleming, the investment bankers,
without any constraints. At the 1988 meeting, however, the
chairman reported that the Investment Panel had considered the
question of ethical investment, and had decided to ask Ethical
Investment Research Services to report twice a year on environmental considerations relevant to the Trust's investments.
Regional Committees were also being asked to report on the
activities of any company that were harmful to the properties of
the Trust.

The Trust's policy appears to have been affected in this case
by a member's question. The extent to which investment policy
has been changed by the reports from Ethical Investment
Research Services has not, however, been reported to members,
so that the effect of the new policy is not known.

4. At the 1989 annual general meeting, a resolution was put forward
asking the Trust to raise funds to purchase land that might be
sold for development by the water authorities after they had
been privatised. The Council replied that it would give high
priority to acquiring water authority land, but that it would not
diverge from its usual criteria for acquisitions. After the
resolution was passed, the Council repeated that water authority
land would be acquired if it was appropriate for the Trust to own
it. In this case, it is not clear if the resolution affected the Trust's
policy, or if there was a danger that the privatised water
companies would sell much land for development.

Public Access to National Trust Land

5. In 1990, a resolution was proposed that urged the Trust to
provide the maximum public access to National Trust land. The
Council agreed that there was room for improvement in the
provisions for access, and accepted the principle of the
resolution. But it pointed out that some restrictions on access
were required where, for example, young trees had been planted
or in nature reserves. The resolution was passed by a large

majority, and the Council promised to set up a group to consider the issue of access. In the 1991 annual report, the Director-General stated that the acquisition of property that improved public access to existing properties would have priority. The report of the group reviewing access was published in 1995; it recommended that better access should be provided but that conservation should continue to have precedence where the two objectives conflicted. It appears that in this case the Trust's policy was marginally changed.

6. In 1992 a resolution was proposed that urged the Trust to set up a fund to compensate tenant farmers for the cost of switching to sustainable husbandry (organic farming methods). Changing to organic methods took three years, it was said, involving a loss of income; rents should therefore be reduced during this period. The Council accepted the spirit of the resolution, and said the Trust already spent £250,000 a year on encouraging environmentally desirable farming methods. It suggested it might be better to set up a fund to encourage environmental objectives in agriculture generally, rather than organic methods specifically. However, in September 1993 the Trust did establish a fund to help farmers convert to organic methods. This resolution may therefore have changed the Trust's policy.

7. In 1995, a resolution was proposed which suggested that the proportion of visitors travelling to National Trust properties by car should be reduced from the present figure of 90 per cent to 60 per cent by 2020, by providing alternative forms of transport to each property. The Council welcomed the resolution, and said it was already acting in its spirit. In the previous four years, it had been working with bus and train operators to provide discounted entry to Trust properties for users of their services. But it also said that the properties should not be made less accessible. In this case it seems that the Trust's policy has been modified by a members' resolution.

This review of some issues raised at National Trust annual general meetings suggests that its management is willing to bend its policy towards the views of its members. What is lacking, however, is evidence in many cases of the magnitude of the effects on the Trust's actions; the Trust does not seem to have a system of reporting back to members on the application of a new policy, such as ethical investment. In other cases, such as the maintenance of the Lake District properties, it is difficult to judge whether the Trust's policy has in practice been affected by the views of members, when they were urging a strengthening of existing policies.

4. The National Trust's Rôle as Landowner

The National Trust became increasingly conscious in the 1990s of its rôle as a landowner seeking to preserve the British countryside, and of the need to consult public opinion if its conservationist policies were to be effectively developed and applied. It therefore launched a review of its countryside policies in 1992, which included opinion surveys of staff and tenants, and involved staff and academics.

The results[11] show the Trust seeking for means of ensuring that its activities in the countryside did benefit the nation, were consistent with contemporary opinion, and were acceptable to the population of the countryside. Its staff still seems to have felt, as had been said a decade before, that the Trust needed to be more outward-looking, more aware of contemporary opinions and of cultural trends, especially attitudes to nature, the past and local heritage. It therefore needed to develop closer links with other organisations in the field of conservation, with academics working on this subject and with residents in the areas where it operated. Consultation with local people who might be affected by the Trust's actions needed to become more formal and effective.

There was also the suggestion that the Trust had a great deal of expertise in conservation, which should be developed, and which could be valuable to other organisations and to other landowners. By promoting and publicising its knowledge, the Trust could influence other landowners, and secure their acceptance of the Trust's practices for the conservation of their property – without the Trust having to acquire the property. There was a feeling that the Trust could and should have more influence on others, and should therefore extend its existing promotional work.

---

[11] *Linking People and Place*, Cirencester: The National Trust, 1995.

Developing the NT's Policy

Policy development was an area in which the Trust's staff felt that improvements were needed. The Trust did not have the expertise in this area possessed by a government department – indeed, the report gives the impression that the Trust was much better equipped to maintain properties and manage land than to develop policies. The report therefore recommended that the Trust should develop a strategy for policy development, research and planning, so that it would be better prepared to react to issues when they arose.

The report shows that the Trust regards its members as one of several groups it treats as partners. It states that it does not formally represent its members, but that membership represents a statement of concern about cultural and environmental degradation. Tenants, who are tied to the Trust by legal agreements, seem to be given a stronger right to be consulted, as are the inhabitants of areas where the Trust owns property. The other groups that the Trust regards as partners are its staff and the volunteers who also work in its properties; other organisations with similar aims; and individuals who are helped by the Trust to contribute to conservation.

5. Conclusions

The National Trust demonstrates that large sums of money can be raised from the public to finance heritage services and the conservation of the countryside. It also shows that most of the people who provide the Trust with money are content to leave decisions about its policy to others, and do not exercise the limited degree of influence that members are given. The rights of members in any British charity are certain to be small, because control is exercised by the trustees; members of the National Trust have more influence than do the supporters of many other charities, who have no opportunity to influence the trustees. But more than 90 per cent of the Trust's members do not want to concern themselves with its policies, and do not use their votes. At the annual general meeting in 1997, members did not propose any resolutions on the Trust's policies.

Members seem to have had some influence over the Trust's policy in the period since 1984, but they have been only one out of several influences. The climate of public opinion on the subjects of heritage and conservation may well have been a stronger influence, although it may often be difficult to separate the two: members are likely to represent public opinion. In the annual report of the Trust for 1979, for example, the Director-General wrote of the greater priority that the Trust was giving to the protection of the countryside and its wildlife. He cited as one reason for this policy that public opinion had, in the previous 10 years, become increasingly focussed on conservation in its broadest sense. This public mood goes back to the early 1960s, and the influence of such books as Rachel Carson's *Silent Spring.*[12] The recent report on *People and Place* shows the Trust to be strongly influenced by current attitudes about the importance of sustainable development and conservation.

The more professional staff the Trust employs, the more likely it is to be influenced by the current climate of opinion. *People and Place* suggests that such influence may be less than might have been expected, because it recommends closer contacts should be developed with academics in relevant specialities. But this report shows that the Trust's staff looked to experts outside the organisation for ideas and information that would improve their performance.

The value of a membership that has a vote may lie in its rôle as a safety valve for public frustration with the managers of an institution like the Trust, and as a threat to the management that they can be publicly warned – or even lose their positions – if they get out of step with public opinion. Annual meetings like that of the Trust, in which members can present resolutions critical of the Trust's policies and vote on the membership of its ruling Council, compel the chairman and management to face up to potentially critical members. This annual test helps to prevent management from becoming complacent or indifferent, and keeps it in touch with public opinion. Dame Jennifer Jenkins has written of her experience of chairing annual general meetings of the Trust: 'Presiding over them was the greatest annual test of nerve and knowledge of the Trust which the chairman had to face.'[13]

Lessons for Public Museums

The interest of the National Trust in the context of the British heritage system is that it is privately financed, very large, relies on

---

[12] Rachel Carson, *Silent Spring*, Boston: Houghton Mifflin, 1962.

[13] Jenkins and James, *op. cit.*, p.314.

private individuals for much of its income, and gives them, its members, some influence over its management. At a time when publicly-owned museums are debating whether to raise some funds from individuals by charging for entrance, the National Trust is raising more than £100 million a year from individuals. The Trust therefore provides living proof that British people are willing to pay to support the national heritage. Each of the 263 properties owned by the Trust and open to the public is a museum that charges for entry.

The publicly-owned museums are charities, like the National Trust. It would not therefore be impossible for them to adopt a constitution like that of the National Trust, in which members are given some influence over the management of the charity in return for an annual contribution to its funds – although legislation would be required. The museums might therefore consider whether it would be desirable to follow the pattern of the National Trust, and invite individuals to contribute towards a museum's costs in return for free entry, the right to elect some of the trustees, and the power to propose advisory resolutions at annual meetings.

Such a policy would only be practicable if the museum could draw a substantial audience, and was prepared to make a significant charge for entry. The Trust's experience does suggest that a season ticket for entry is a stronger attraction for members than the right to vote. But a minority of well-informed members can be an effective force for the good if they have the opportunity to question management at annual meetings and can vote some trustees out of office. It might have been salutary, for example, for the trustees of the British Museum to have had to defend before an informed audience their decision to reduce expenditure on acquisitions rather than to introduce admission charges.

The National Trust is the most successful British institution in the heritage field. It offers lessons that can usefully be learned by other institutions that wish to add private to public sources of funds.

6

MUSEUMS AND GALLERIES: STOREHOUSES OF VALUE?

Sir Gerald Elliot

Former Chairman, Scottish Arts Council

Museums, Galleries and Economics

MUSEUMS AND ART GALLERIES ARE a particular segment of the cultural spectrum which has managed to keep itself remarkably free from the probing questions of economic analysis. They are often thought to enshrine values which cannot be expressed in material terms and certainly not brought into the market-place. They are also considered to be appropriate institutions to be financed collectively through the public purse and not by charges on people for access. This was reflected in Britain in the 1845 Act, which empowered government, local and central, to set up museums 'for the instruction and education of the inhabitants'.

Public munificence does not remove economic issues. Even if government provided all the funds required by museums they would have to assess the allocation of resources to alternative uses within their spheres of responsibility. However, they also get substantial support from private sources in both cash and objects donated, and entrance charges to the public are gradually being introduced. Lastly, and perhaps most important, the museums are repositories of millions of objects, and constantly acquiring more. These collections may be considered 'priceless' within the museums, but in the world outside many of the items have defined market prices. The estate which they comprise is of enormous money value, and should be managed in the most effective way possible.

As we grow more conscious of our history and culture we become more interested in museums. There are already over 2,500 museums in Britain, and the number grows every year, covering almost every area of human interest, fine arts, local life, religion, defunct industries, social customs, etc. Many of these museums, with limited collections, survive with a good deal of voluntary work and

117

little, if any, public money. The bigger museums and galleries, which do depend largely on public money, have a broader rôle, not just to educate and instruct but also as general repositories of culture and history recorded through material objects, and even sometimes as the expression of national purpose and identity. This paper will suggest how our larger institutions can use the economic system of which they are inevitably a part to carry out better the purposes for which they were set up.

The trustees and directors of our national museums and galleries are well aware of these economic issues but not always keen to tackle them. They believe they are preserving collections of objects of a value to the country's citizens which cannot and should not be expressed in money terms, and feel that any attempt to put money values on them is misplaced. They are, however, as in most other human organisations, faced with the need to use the resources they are given in accordance with the values set by the market. Buildings must be put up and maintained, staff hired, objects acquired, exhibited and stored. They cannot avoid relating the non-material values which they seek to foster to the material values with which they must work.

Intense interest in conserving the objects of the past has tended to dominate the policies of museum and gallery boards. This has led, until recently, to more stress on the curating function than on the job of education and instruction. Correspondingly, museum directors have an appetite for acquiring objects which is rarely satiated. With due discrimination for quality, almost every object can be judged an important part of cultural or social history which should be given a museum home for fear of its being lost or destroyed. There have been some spectacular battles in Britain in recent years between those who look on museums as repositories and research centres for culture and those who believe they should be more concerned with the education and entertainment of the citizen.

The primary funding for acquisition of objects by these institutions, whether they be world-famous sculptures or four-million-year-old fossil skeletons, comes from government purchase grants, but those slender provisions are far exceeded by the availability of money from other government funds, voluntary charities and private gifts. The most valuable of such gifts come, as they have in the past, from private individuals who have built up collections and who pass them on before or after death to the state, generously conveying to their fellow citizens the opportunity to share the pleasures they have enjoyed.

An active acquisitions policy by museums should be welcomed. Closed unchanging collections lose public interest and cease to stimulate. However, even as simple repositories museums cannot be allowed to grow for ever. Exhibition space will run out, public interest will reach its limits and museums will become gigantic warehousing operations. Policies for disposal to match acquisition will be needed sooner or later. Such policies come up against a strong tradition in the museum world that objects once acquired must always remain.

The Doctrine of Accession

The doctrine of accession, similar, in the passion with which it is held, to the beliefs which split the early Christian churches, is to the effect that an object which has once passed into the ownership of a museum or gallery is endowed with a sanctity which cannot be taken from it. It should only be deprived of its status and sold, or transferred elsewhere, by a formal process of de-accessioning, and that should be limited to exceptional circumstances.

Accessionism still has strong support in Europe, though it has been waning in the USA. It seems to be a belief adopted by virtually all professionals in museums and galleries. If they had to swear a Hippocratic oath on entering their professions, this would be part of it. They support their stance by various arguments. You must never sell works of art from a public museum, they say, because you cannot be sure that your judgement in selling is right. They may seem unimportant items to your trustees now, but a future generation may have quite different views. It may turn out that the dross you are disposing of now would have been jewels of the collection in 50 years' time. The argument is supported by selected horror stories from the USA, where boards of galleries have lived to regret bitterly disposals made by their less enlightened predecessors. Good judgement, however, applies as much to acquisition as to disposal. If museum directors have so little confidence in their own judgement that they do not dare to sell any items from their collections, they should be equally reluctant to buy anything.

It is the dominant spirit of the scholar-curators that maintains rampant accessionism. They believe the essential function of collections is to bring together all objects that can contribute to the pursuit of knowledge, with exhibition to the public as a secondary matter. Their argument, carried to its limit, would be that galleries and museums require, for history and reference purposes, to have in their possession not only examples of every artist, craftsman, fossil, astrolabe, harvesting machine, and so on, but also, unless they are strict duplicates, as many specimens of each that they can get hold of. Everything is potentially valuable for research. They suggest an analogue with the copyright libraries, where every published work is to be found. That view might just be maintained within a small selected cultural range, but in a world overwhelmed by objects, all of which have some claim to be collected and preserved, a policy of unlimited acquisition is quite untenable.

Accessionism is most powerfully applied to great paintings and sculptures of the past. They have come to be considered the prime embodiments of Western culture, developed through the Greeks and the Roman Empire. Their outstanding place in aesthetic values, reflected by their high money worth in the market-place, encourages their acquisition and sanctification. Sometimes they are wrapped in a patriotic flag, but more as symbols of national power than because of native origin. In the National Gallery of Scotland, the Poussins, El Grecos and Turners have no Scottish affiliation, but their possession confers prestige on Scotland. It is not surprising that such treasures should be considered the inalienable patrimony of a country, even though they would sit equally comfortably as someone else's patrimony. This possessiveness for art objects can get carried too far. We are being continually asked to 'save for the nation' one or other great work of art which was brought out of the Continent of Europe some time during the last three centuries to adorn a British nobleman's country house, and must now be sold. Such a work can hardly be considered part of our national heritage.

The idea of national heritage becomes even more tenuous if we are contemplating collections from past civilisations – Egyptian mummies for example – which clearly play an important part in another country's history and might well be claimed as part of its heritage. The doctrine is a comfortable one for the countries of Europe, which have been able in recent centuries to acquire some of the world's finest treasures. It is less happy for the countries outside, who came late into the game. The outstanding symbols of their past civilisations were long ago shipped to Europe, and their collecting activities stretch back only a few decades. Our cultural selfishness, spiced with imperialism, sits uneasily in a world where we seek to encourage culture, like trade, to flow freely over national boundaries. If the Getty Foundation wants another Leonardo and confirms this by the high price it is prepared to pay, need this be a national disaster for the country from which it migrates? People appreciate art in California too and we might with a good grace share 'our' treasures. Museum directors and art lobbies would do better to keep their money for purchases in a free international market rather than strive to fence in for themselves a doubtful national heritage.

The Influence of 'Accessionism'

The influence of the accessionist doctrine is still strong in Britain. That is shown clearly in the registration scheme run by the Museums and Galleries Commission (MGC), which provides assistance and a little funding to smaller museums in Britain. Under this scheme museums undertake to maintain high standards of exhibition and conservation and in return benefit from advice, technical services and sometimes grants from the MGC. The scheme also lays down principles of acquisition and disposal policy. The disposal policy is not dogmatic and can be stretched, but it does state that *'unless each museum governing body accepts the principle of "strong presumption against disposal", the whole purpose of the museum is called into question'*. Expanding on this policy the guidelines state that:

> 'Decisions to dispose of items will not be made with the principal aim of generating funds. Once a decision to dispose of an item has been taken, priority will be given to retaining the item within the public domain and with this in view it will be offered first, by exchange, gift or sale to registered museums before disposal to other interested individuals or organisations is considered.'

These provisions could no doubt be circumvented by a determined museum board, but it would certainly be discouraged by the intention of the MGC that any constructive disposal to raise money for improvement of the collection should be frustrated. It is not clear from the guidelines why a considered disposal policy is held to call the whole purpose of a museum into question or why the MGC feels unable to trust the museums' boards to make their own decisions on disposal.

The MGC view is clearly influenced by the UK Museums Association which has published Ethical Guidelines on Disposal (June 1996). There we find an expansion of the MGC guidelines, for example:

- 2A: 'As a key function of a museum is to preserve a collection in perpetuity, there is a strong presumption against the disposal of any item from a museum's permanent collection'; and

- 2E: 'Disposal should never be undertaken principally for financial reasons (either to raise money for any purpose or to reduce expenditure). Selling an item from a museum's permanent collection out of the public domain always risks damaging public confidence in museums and is, therefore, a course of action that the Museums Association Ethics Committee would never recommend. In addition, society benefits from the long tradition of mutual co-operation between museums. Selling, rather than giving, items to other registered museums jeopardises this tradition and is therefore not recommended.'

This negative code, even though modified by some wise advice about how to make disposals acceptable to donors and supporters of the museum, blocks on dubious principles the benefits which museums could gain by the unlocking of some of their unused resources.

Direct government policy on disposals, to the extent it has been articulated, is similar. The National Heritage (Scotland) Act 1985, which sets down the constitution of the National Museums of Scotland and the National Galleries of Scotland, gives very limited powers of disposal to these bodies, though the loopholes left suggest that Ministers at the time saw that disposal policy might have to be loosened in the future.

Behind the MGC policy lies the fear that, if such controls are not applied, collections will dwindle and eventually disappear. The experience of recent years in Britain is that, far from shrinking, there has been a spontaneous expansion in museums and galleries, led by enthusiasts and supported by public interest. The accessionists also seem to hold the superstition that objects once disposed of by their galleries cease to exist. That is patently not so. They go into other collections, where they may be better exhibited, or into private hands, where they will be well looked after and no doubt appear in the market again later. Accession condemns museums and galleries to stagnating collections, unable to change except by the small increments allowed through their government purchase grants and the erratic favours of private donors.

The doctrine of the sacredness of art objects is not confined to museum directors. Several British universities, finding themselves short of funds for their tasks of education and research, have sought to sell works of art in their ownership. This has raised a storm of protest from within and without the universities. The universities, it is argued, are the appointed guardians of civilised values, and by selling works of art they are renouncing their traditions of enlightened learning. There is no logic in this view. Universities are not museums. Their work is in the nourishment of knowledge, not in the collection of art objects. They may have deliberately built up specialist collections or have acquired them fortuitously by gift, but these are rarely integral to the university's work. There is no good reason why such collections, and other art objects which have come into its hands, should not be passed on or varied from time to time in accordance with the needs and priorities of the university. It is the sanctity conferred on art objects, linked closely to their market value, which makes university authorities cower in the face of what they consider to be public opinion. At Edinburgh University there was controversy about the sale of a De Vries bronze and a painting by Jacob Ruzdael, each of considerable value, the bronze on public display but ignored within the university, the picture on loan and hung in the National Gallery of Scotland. These two items were part of a bequest made to the university about 200 years ago. Any disposal would of course have to have been in accordance with the provisions of the trust concerned, or a variance agreed by the courts. The university eventually decided to drop the matter, as there continued to be internal hostility to a disposal and the immediate financial crisis had been overcome. It did, however, seem wrong that a transaction which could have benefited both education and art appreciation should have been lost in this way.

The National Arts Collection Fund (NACF), a private charity which assists the purchase of art objects for collections, played a part in this controversy. It threatened the university that if it persisted in selling the two works of art, the Fund would no longer support its art collections, such as the well-known Galpin collection of musical instruments. The justification given for this high-handed attitude was that any sale of art objects previously donated to the university would, regardless of circumstances, seriously affect the national flow of bequests and gifts on which collections so much depended. This argument, as discussed below, is a thin one, and the morality of trying to force a policy on the university in an area quite outside the NACF's remit was dubious.

Effects of Inalienability

If art and museum objects are inalienable and acquisitions of new objects continues steadily, a collection will soon outstrip its exhibition capacity. The Royal Museum of Scotland in Edinburgh, although it is expanding its capacity with a new building, cannot exhibit publicly more than 10 per cent of its stock, though it can claim that a number of its objects now in store are for the purpose of reference and research rather than exhibition. The costs of storage for a museum are high, since many exhibits require air-conditioning and a bunch of unique objects of varying bulk and weight cannot be handled with the efficiency of a modern store house. Unless the accumulation of objects is reversed the costs of storage and maintenance of stock will make increasingly heavy, and perhaps intolerable, demands on museum budgets.

The National Gallery of Scotland has been seeking to build a new gallery in Glasgow, not because there is a pressing demand from the public to enjoy more pictures, but because it has in store a large number of works which it has never been able to exhibit. Manchester Art Gallery, on receiving recently a large lottery award to extend its premises, has declared that it will now be able to exhibit 50 per cent of its fine art and 30 per cent of its decorative art. Galleries are increasingly popular, and it may be that a large frustrated demand for more gallery space could be shown by trends in visitor numbers, but gallery policy should be decided by considerations other than simply the availability in store of second-order art objects.

In a world where art objects are vigorously bought and sold in an open market, a museum or gallery director promoting the culture of permanent possession is unhappily placed. He seeks to use his meagre purchase grant to get the best aesthetic or historic value he can for the money, but he is in competition with other institutions all over the world, many far better endowed than his own, and with private collectors, some of whom are more interested in speculative investment than cultural quality. Because he and his kindred can only buy and never sell, the market steadily hardens against them. The objects taken up by private collectors may appear again in the market in the next generation when the owner dies or gets bored with them. Those purchased by museums, however, are permanently put out of circulation, so the available stock of desirable objects is being steadily diminished, with consequent increase in their price. The Getty Museum in California, with an endowment to purchase works of art on a huge scale, has dismayed the directors of European galleries, who can always be outbid and see prices constantly pushed upwards.

The sensible commercial reaction to a scarcity and rising prices is to keep out of the market and hope that the fashion cycle will bring values down again in due course, while looking at other sources of supply which can provide close substitutes. This of course does happen. French impressionists peaked in value some years ago, as a Japanese insurance company which invested in a Van Gogh found to its pain, and gallery directors do spread their interest to less highly priced artists, dead or alive, encouraged by the art trade which works vigorously in every way it can to expand demand. It is difficult, however, for directors to take a strong line against the judgements of the market, even though their aesthetic views may point in different directions. They are inevitably influenced by the prevailing consensus, and their patrons and the viewing public expect them generally to follow it. The Canova sculpture, 'The Three Graces', bought by the Victoria & Albert Museum and the Scottish National Gallery for £8 million, was promoted by these galleries, and supported by the various funding bodies which contributed, much less for its intrinsic aesthetic value than because it was a recognised art ikon, given status by its enormous market price alone, and expected both to reflect some glory on the galleries acquiring it and to attract crowds to see it.

That particular acquisition is a good example of the harm caused by high collecting/low disposal policies steered by the commercial market. 'The Three Graces' is a fine piece of sculpture, though not everyone is convinced of its outstanding aesthetic merit. It was about to be sold from a private collection and an appeal was made for it to be preserved for the nation. The National Gallery of Scotland decided that, despite (perhaps because of) the high price required, this was a priority for purchase, and eventually it was triumphantly acquired, in conjunction with the Victoria & Albert Museum and with the help of the NACF, National Heritage Memorial Fund and private donors. The idea of time-share applied to works of art is a good one, increasing the numbers of the public who can see the work. It might well be applied on a broader scale, spreading ownership among several museums, though this would discomfort curators, who like to have full ownership and control of their objects. Despite this the NGS had to devote the whole of its purchase fund for the year to 'The Three Graces', as well as drawing heavily on its goodwill with the supporting bodies and donors. It is difficult to believe that the huge sum involved could not have been used far more fruitfully to strengthen the NGS collections in other ways. It might also be noted that the NGS was at the time complaining of shortage of funds to run its galleries properly.

Working With the Market

When museum and gallery collections are already so dependent on the market-place it seems perverse that their boards do not allow it to work to their advantage as well as to their disadvantage. If boards were free to sell from their collections items which were duplicates or which did not conform to the parameters set for the collection, for instance in type, historic period or quality, considerable funds could be made available to buy objects which the collection really needed. Collections could be strengthened and gaps filled. Instead of being universal magpies, museums would be more able to adopt discriminating policies and carry them out by judicious buying and selling. Nor should they be concerned that what they sell may break out of the charmed museum circle and pass again into private hands. There is no reason why great paintings, like great houses, should not pass part of their lifespan in the ownership of individuals or indeed of other institutions such as industrial companies, where they will give at least as much pleasure and enlightenment as they would in the cellars of a museum. One important effect of generally adopted de-accessioning policies would be a drop in the art and antiquities market, painful to speculative investors but of great value to the collecting institutions, working in a market where supply was no longer throttled.

The current dogma condemns any disposal of objects even when the money is used to replace them by more suitable ones. It is even more hostile to the idea of selling valuable pieces to raise money for other purposes, such as improving museum facilities. That too should be challenged. Art objects are publicly collected for the benefit of people. They require to be properly presented to give the instruction and stimulation which is their purpose. Is one Picasso among many so sacred that it cannot be sold to provide money (say) for a new gallery space? The MGC does leave the door open for such virement (a good Arts Council term), but since its guidelines if strictly applied make it very difficult for museums to get any money from disposals the prospect is remote.

Realising the Value of Museum Stocks

Professor Bruno Frey recently pointed out the immense value in money terms of the stocks of art and cultural treasures lying in the vaults of museums.[1] We should be asking, he says, whether that value, which is not even providing a return by giving viewers enjoyment in exhibition, should not be used to give the nation, which owns it, benefit in other ways. It would be salutary if each national museum was asked to publish in its yearly report, like a commercial company, an approximate assessment of the value of all the assets, including the collections which had been entrusted to it. That would bring home to the board, and to the public, the heavy, and hitherto undeclared, responsibilities of museums, and bring their boards to consider whether they could use part of the sleeping values revealed to fulfil better the objectives they and their government patrons have set for themselves.

The doctrine of inalienability came out strongly when the Scottish Arts Council (SAC) a few years ago set out to disperse its collection of pictures and sculpture, built up over 40 years, on the grounds that it was not required as an historic record, and that the money spent on circulating the collection, mainly lending pictures out to business and public offices, together with the capital value if it was sold, could be better used in other ways to promote contemporary art, which was one of the Arts Council's functions. That proposal raised wide protests. Artists whose work had been bought by the SAC claimed that their trust was being betrayed and their status demeaned by the proposed sale of the works. Art historians declared

---

[1] Bruno S. Frey, 'Cultural Economics and Museum Behaviour', *Scottish Journal of Political Economy*, Vol. 41, No. 3, August 1994, p. 325.

that the collection was unique in recording the changing buying fashions of the period, and commercial gallery owners predicted a collapse of the art market. Behind it all was the firm belief held by practitioners of art, if not by citizens, that art objects should enjoy certain rights of public establishment which isolate them from the normal exercise of choice and preference through the market. The SAC retreated at the time, but has now succeeded in dispersing its collections to museums and other public bodies, though without the financial benefit it could have gained by selling some of its items.

The restrictive view of museum and gallery property has concentrated on art galleries and museums which have objects of high value, however defined, and might be described as national collections. Below this level there are many small specialised museums. Those institutions often house objects of low market value, in common use yesterday if not today, and easily replaceable by similar things. They do not have the same defensiveness about their collections and can contemplate without emotion the trading of part of their stock to improve their displays. If they are forced to follow strict accessionist policies, as laid down in the guidelines of the MGC, their collections, in the same way as larger collections, may be condemned to an immobility which denies their function.

Private Gifts and Legacies

Much of the museum and gallery collections have been put together not by purchase but from the gifts and legacies of private people. The Wallace collection in London came to the nation by a single legacy, likewise the Burrell collection in Glasgow. Donors realise their collections will not survive them and, rather than contemplate dispersal under the hammer, prefer that they should pass to the public domain, giving at the same time some immortality to their names. Besides the large donors there are thousands of people who pass on their smaller treasures with the pleasure of improving public collections. Government contributes by accepting works of art in lieu of estate duty on death.

This generosity provides continuous help in enlarging the stock of museums and institutions, but creates its own problems. Such gifts are never free. They are rarely accompanied by an endowment for the extra storage and exhibition space required, and the gift may be hedged with such conditions that make one suspect that it is made more for the satisfaction of the donor's personal desires than for its contribution to the public weal. Sir William Burrell, in donating his famous collection of art to Glasgow, set conditions for its housing and treatment, with the intention of giving proper protection to these valuable objects. However, it took 30 years before Glasgow Council could provide premises satisfactory to the trustees, and the provisions forbidding lending to other museums are now causing embarrassment and are being challenged. A British collector, Sir Denis Mahon, has recently passed a collection of highly valued French pictures to the NACF, to be lent to galleries at its discretion, but apparently with the rider that they are to be withdrawn from any gallery which imposes admission charges or sells any items of its collections. We should hope that galleries will not be influenced in their policies by this crude pressure, which detracts substantially from the value of the gift. Galleries are so anxious to add to their collections that they find it difficult to reject donations with strings attached, but they may be laying up trouble for themselves if they accept them.

Gifts are generally assumed to be inalienable whether or not that is specified by the donor. No benefactor will be pleased if his art objects, to which he may have had a strong emotional attachment, are accepted by a museum and appear a few years later in the auction room. It is this fear that makes fund-giving bodies in Britain so sensitive about selling anything. The NACF and the MGC both maintain that if museums adopt an active selling policy, the flow of gifts will dry up. Bequests will go elsewhere, to places where an eternal home can be guaranteed, or they will not be made at all. That is the instinctive reaction of the museum professional, intent on increasing his collection at any cost. It seems, however, more likely that the prospective benefactor will make his dispositions to museums regardless of their selling policies, provided that he has assurances that his treasures will be kept undisturbed for a reasonable period. Such a period might be a maximum of 25 years; it would hardly be responsible for a government or museum to guarantee a longer period, and permanent guardianship would be an obligation that it might be unable to fulfil. If the conditions of acceptance of bequests are spelled out in this way, as they should be, some donors may withdraw. That would be a loss worth incurring to ensure that museums were not burdened with unwanted and inalienable property in the future. In any case, a more liberal policy in the buying and selling of museum properties is not likely to influence the donor if the conditions attached to his own property are clear and satisfactory.

The NACF, which collects large amounts of private contributions and contributes to the purchase of art objects for museums and galleries, is doing invaluable work and deserves every encouragement. However, it should devote the energy with which it fights all disposals to convincing donors that well-planned disposal policies must be one of the functions of good museums and that donations can still sit honourably within them.

A subsidiary argument against disposals (used by the chairman of NACF in correspondence with Edinburgh University) is that the raising of money by that method would get the government 'off the hook' – in other words, simply relieve government of its funding obligations. That argument is a hardy annual to discourage any form of non-government finance and has been vigorously used against every sort of new project designed to obtain more outside money for arts and culture. Commercial sponsorship, entrance charges for museums, and gallery shops can all be condemned in this way. It has of course recently been government policy to reduce dependence on public funding. That might be cut as private funding increased, though the power of the arts lobby would probably be sufficient to prevent a reduction in real terms in public provision. It would be suicidal to assume that government will cover any increased funding demands and that contributions from other sources will simply be cancelled out by withdrawal of government patronage.

Every museum and gallery depends enormously on private generosity. There is a continuous flow of donated objects into the large national institutions, and the smaller new museums that are continually being set up depend almost entirely for their initial stock on private enthusiasm. Museum and gallery buildings are also considered to be suitable objects of benevolence by the wealthy. They are generally welcomed with gratitude and they provide a permanent visible memorial for the donors. We in Britain have benefited in recent years from Sainsbury, Sackler and many others. There are, however, dangers in private donations which are harnessed to publicly financed institutions. Apart from the extra costs to the receiving museum in storing and exhibiting its gifts, they may upset the balance in the collection which the board is aiming for and push the museum in quite a different direction from that intended. A museum's yearly grant for purchases may be small, but at least it focuses the board's attention on alternative choices within a limited sum of money and forces it to devise a collecting policy and deliberately carry it out. A disposal policy linked to an acquisitions policy would give the board real power to control its collection to the public's benefit, with the whims of its donors playing only a minor part.

'Free Gifts' ...and the Effects of Lottery Money

Free gifts must be welcome but only if they harmonise with the criteria which museums and galleries, with the guidance of their public guardians, set for themselves. In the same way, free gifts from government outside its normal financing should be cheered, but with reservation. The national lottery has suddenly provided for arts projects sums of money beyond the wildest dreams of promoters. Up to recently, eligibility has been limited to buildings and there has been a requirement to find some private funds to match, but these are being modified as the supply of credible propositions and of matching funds dries up. Whereas the allocation of government funds to museums and galleries, both for yearly operating and for capital expenditure is scrutinised, however roughly, against allocation to alternative arts and culture purposes, and, more widely, against alternative non-cultural uses of the money (say for education or sport), lotteries money is not exposed to even that rigour. Most cultural organisations adopt some sort of policy guidelines as to their size and scope, in which the aspirations of their directors are tempered by the disciplines imposed by those who finance them, whether the Treasury, private contributions, or the market in the form of the public paying directly for access. If large sums of money are made available to which these disciplines do not apply, the result may well be an expansion of arts facilities well beyond any level decided by government policy or the demands of the public. Such expansion is not free. Any new facilities in buildings carry with them new costs of operation, and whatever the bland assurances given by the promoters, these costs are likely to have to be covered in the future by the public purse.

Government has in recent years been cautious about providing capital for expanding the national museums and galleries for which it is financially responsible, particularly where the institutions themselves are reluctant to obtain money from the public direct by charging entrance fees. During the 1980s Scottish ministers were lobbied strongly by the board of the Royal Museum of Scotland to provide capital for a new wing to house a Museum of Scotland. They eventually agreed to do so, but only if a substantial part of the total costs was raised by public appeal. That was a rough way of checking that there was broad public interest in the project which could be shown in money terms. A few years later the National Galleries of Scotland put forward its schemes for expansion. These were not so clear-cut in their justification and were further fogged by rivalry between Edinburgh and Glasgow for the site. Government declined to provide capital funds, and the project would probably have been shelved if the newly established lottery funds had not opened an alternative source of money. The new gallery, finally to be sited in Glasgow, still, after three years of debate, has to win the lottery money it needs, though it seems likely to do so. The tortuous history of the project illustrates how the assessment of public funding of museums and galleries by some sort of benefit criterion is upset by the windfall appearance of large sums of 'free' money.

Entrance Charges

The remaining area for financing museums and galleries lies in entrance charges for the public. This has been a contentious issue in Britain. Government has until recently pressed boards to introduce charges and many of them have stoutly resisted. Professionals have set out freedom of entry as a main principle of policy, though they have been ready to break it by charging fees for special exhibitions which could not be put on without that source of income. It is difficult to see much defence for the no-charge policy other than tradition. The benefits given by great galleries and museums are considerable, but not so strong that they require to be placed in a different category from the many other forms of instruction and entertainment for which we expect people to pay. Some parts of these benefits can be found elsewhere. There are close substitutes in books, reproductions, or TV programmes. There must be few people whose lives would be seriously affected because they could not afford to or did not care to pay a museum entry fee. The free entry advocates can, of course, point to a marked decline in visitor numbers wherever entry charges have been introduced. That is only to be expected, and says nothing about the extent of benefit lost for those who decide to forgo entry rather than pay a fee. People do not visit free museums always in pursuit of culture. The main hall of the Royal Scottish Museum in Edinburgh provides, amongst other amenities, a large space for children to play in on wet Sunday afternoons, and a warm waiting room for those attending the proceedings of the Sheriff Court opposite. Recently introduced entrance fees may make it less attractive.

Any benefit lost through the introduction of entry charges and a reduction of visitors should be balanced against the improvements which the new stream of income can allow the museums to undertake. Entry charges will have the same effect to be seen wherever a free service is turned into a paying one. The organisation, once it appreciates that its prosperity will depend directly on attracting visitors and satisfying their requirements, will become much more sensitive to its responsibilities for educating, instructing and indeed entertaining our citizens. This would also help the assessment of the curating and reference function as a separate though overlapping activity, perhaps to be financed on different criteria.

The direct linkage of the museums by entry charges to those who appreciate them can only raise standards, encourage effective operation, and stimulate them to creative activity. Our tradition of free museums and galleries is a brave and generous gesture, but seems in today's world to have little or no effect in advancing the general level of culture of our citizens, as it was intended to do. That policy is closely associated with the reverential view of museum objects. Once we accept that these institutions cannot and should not be isolated from the beneficial workings of the market system, these dogmas may disappear altogether.

Our national museums and galleries are fine institutions. In recent years the efforts of many in government and within the institutions themselves have brought them to play a more vigorous part in our cultural life, while still remaining essential repositories of the past. With more focused acquisition and disposal policies, a more discriminating attitude towards donors and the stimulus of entry charges they could serve us still better.

7

INTERNATIONAL ASPECTS OF

HERITAGE POLICIES

Dick Netzer

New York University

Introduction

THE SUBSTANTIAL DEMAND FOR CULTURAL HERITAGE SERVICES that are physically available only at great distances from one's place of residence – in other countries – has been apparent at least since St. Helena claimed to have discovered the site of the Crucifixion and the True Cross, and had the Church of the Holy Sepulchre built on that site, in the 4th century AD. In the following centuries, untold thousands of pilgrims have travelled great distances to that and other religious sites that have become important elements of the planet's cultural heritage, and provided a considerable share of the financial support for their preservation, such as it is. More recent pilgrims lean to the secular. In the last 200 years, the intellectuals and artists among European and North American visitors to Venice transformed the city from a shabby relic of a shattered tyranny into the most prominent of modern Western cultural symbols. The visitors became obsessed with the need to preserve the dying city, and had a major rôle in doing so.[1] Today, with cheap air travel, foreigners flock to hundreds of other heritage sites and provide a good deal of the financial support their preservation requires. That international demand and its satisfaction is the subject of this chapter.

Like the local and national demand for heritage services, the international demand may not be fully reflected in market transactions between consumers and providers of heritage services, and therefore may not yield providers enough revenue to assure the

---

[1] The story is elegantly told in a recent book: John Pemble, *Venice Rediscovered*, Oxford: Oxford University Press, 1995.

degree of preservation and protection that consumers seek. The standard externality arguments apply to the international interest in heritage, as well as to the national and local interest. Those arguments are a mixed bag, from the national and local perspective, but appear to be somewhat more robust in the case of the international demand.

In part, that is because the income elasticity of demand for heritage preservation appears to be quite high, and much of the heritage for which there is trans-national demand is located in countries that are not rich, or at least not rich relative to the costs of preservation of their vast stocks of heritage. Therefore, both market transactions and action by the local and national authorities may fall short of reflecting the international demand.

There are some strong parallels between protection of the cultural heritage and protection of the natural environment at the trans-national spatial scale. In both cases, there are likely to be some cases of market failure, as well as cases in which local and national governments fail, either by omission or by pursuing policies that favour local concerns that are hostile to preservation, such as refusing to recognise the degradation that may occur with congestion.

The chapter concludes with a discussion of mechanisms for accommodating the international demand for heritage services, a discussion set in the framework of 'fiscal federalism', or, to use the faddish and misleading word, 'subsidiarity', that is, the assignment of responsibility for action and finance to the appropriate tier of governmental authority.

Externalities and Heritage Demand

The markets for heritage services are characterised by various well-known local, or non-geographic, failures, which also apply to the demand on the part of foreigners; there are spatial externalities in addition. The conventional concerns are for types of demand that are not reflected in market transactions. In the language of Frey and Pommerehne,[2] there are types of value that are close to impossible to internalise within the markets for cultural goods and services, including heritage services: *option value* for potential use of cultural

---

[2]   Bruno S. Frey and Werner W. Pommerehne, *Muses & Markets: Explorations in the Economics of the Arts,* Oxford: Basil Blackwell, 1989, p. 19.

services; *existence value*, that is, utility from awareness of the existence of cultural goods and services that one does not directly use; *bequest value*, for future generations; *prestige value* for those who may have little interest in art as such; and *education value* in fostering creativity, the capacity for cultural evaluation and aesthetic standards and, more concretely, talents and skills useful in the mass media and other industries. Surveys in Australia and Canada and referenda results in Switzerland strongly suggest that, at least in those countries, such demand is real for ordinary consumers and voters.

As with all claims that there are benefits external to market transactions that we should worry about, in connection with services that do involve trading in markets, one needs to be sceptical of these claims. The claimed benefits are sometimes imaginary, at other times real but trivial in magnitude, and at still other times adequately produced as a necessary by-product of market transactions. In some cases, the benefits are external to market transaction largely because the services are under-priced, by fiat. But there is at least some reality to the claims.

It is difficult to believe that foreigners could care much about prestige value of heritage in a country not their own, and perhaps they can be expected to be largely indifferent to the educational value, the benefits of which are captured by the residents of the country where the services are provided. However, there must be many cases in which foreigners would be willing to pay handsomely for the degree and scope of heritage services that will generate option, existence and bequest values. At first blush, it might seem that the total demand for these values on the part of foreigners should be quite small relative to the demand on the part of residents of the country or of the city that is the site of the heritage element. The barrier of travel distance should reduce option value for foreigners, because the option seems so much less likely to be exercised by foreigners than by locals. That also should apply to bequest value: the grandchildren of foreigners will have a more attenuated connection with heritage than the grandchildren of locals. Existence value is real only to the extent that consumers are aware that the heritage element actually does exist. Distance surely affects this awareness. Perhaps no more than one in a thousand New Yorkers is aware of the identity and existence of the few buildings in the city that are more than 200 years old, but they probably outnumber by a factor of 100 the foreigners who are similarly aware.[3]

But economic demand equals the number of would-be purchasers multiplied by the prices they are willing to pay, and it is conceivable, perhaps even likely, that the intensity of the demand for non-marketable heritage values on the part of foreigners is vastly greater than that of locals, in many cases. In part, this is simply because people who travel long distances are likely to be relatively rich. In part, it simply reflects the influence of travel costs on the relative valuation visitors place on the attractions of destinations: for the past 40 years, it has been well-established that travel costs afford a good proxy for travellers' valuations of the attractions of natural sites.

A rather different class of externality comes from the literature of fiscal federalism. Outsiders may value highly services that are produced in part or wholly by governmental action and finance. Because they have no political voice in public decision-making in other countries, they have no way to express their willingness to pay for those valued services. Meanwhile, local people who do have a political voice, will support only the services that *they* value highly. Thus, a level of heritage services justified by the aggregate demand for the services may not be provided, if there is a major degree of indivisibility or continuousness in the production of the service. Once again, because those foreigners are likely to be relatively rich, their *per capita* demand for heritage services may be a large multiple of the *per capita* demand of locals.

The reality of this unmet demand has been amply demonstrated over the years by the financial support for heritage protection in distant places, by individuals, philanthropic organisations and governments in Europe and North America.

Rich Heritage and Poor Countries

Although there is no obvious correlation across countries between the supply of heritage sites and *per capita* GDP, it is a fact that there are extremely poor countries with a rich stock of heritage, like Cambodia and Burma, and very rich countries with relatively modest stocks of heritage, like the USA and Canada. The demand

---

[3] There are only five such buildings, one dating from the 17th century and four from the 18th century.

for heritage services is clearly income-elastic, as centuries of history have demonstrated, both within and across countries. Rich rulers and individuals in relatively poor countries have been willing to spend large amounts for heritage services, for example, in Russia and Poland in the 18th century, and lavish support for heritage has been especially pronounced in the countries that were among the richest in their eras, like France and Great Britain in the 18th and 19th centuries. In recent years, government heritage expenditure *per capita* in European countries does appear to have been highly correlated with *per capita* GDP. The implication, of course, is that there must be demand for heritage services in numerous poor countries on the part of people who live in rich countries which will be undersupplied by normal market and governmental decision-making processes.

The issue is not simply one of absolute poverty, but of the stock of heritage relative to GDP. A country may have a high income, but if its stock of heritage is extremely large, the law of diminishing marginal utility will apply: consumers and voters will value the 10,000th 18th-century country house less than they value the 1,000th. Moreover, to the extent that the government must finance heritage services, a vast stock of heritage to be protected confronts the problem of the deadweight losses from taxation. A well-known corollary in the theory of optimal taxation is that such losses increase more than proportionally (probably exponentially) with the rate of taxation. So, it is almost certain that if the costs of the full protection of all of the heritage are equal to a high fraction of GDP even in a rich country, such protection will not be forthcoming and the supply of heritage services will diminish over time, as heritage elements decay and eventually disappear from the stock. Foreigners may be willing to provide some of the finance needed to minimise the losses, but they need mechanisms to do so.

USA and Italy Compared

In an earlier paper, I made some extremely crude and rather arbitrary comparisons of the US and Italy with respect to the ratio of annual heritage capital consumption to GDP.[4] Extrapolating from

---

4   Dick Netzer, 'Gross National Product and the Cultural Endowment of Nations', paper presented at the Autumn Seminar on 'The Value of Cultural Goods', International Center for Research in Arts Economics, Venice, December 1992.

data on the insurance carried by art museums, I estimated that the total value of works of art owned by museums and by private parties in the US may have been no more than $60 billion at year-end 1989, only 1·1 per cent of GDP. This suggests that, if this form of capital – much of it well-protected in museums and even in private collections, and a good deal of it not terribly old – depreciates at the slow rate of 0·5 per cent per year, capital consumption allowances are well under 1/100th of 1 per cent of GDP in the US.[5] In the national wealth estimates for the United States, the total value, at current costs, of the stock of government and privately-owned structures at year-end 1989 was set at just under $4,900 billion.[6] A generous estimate would be that the value of non-residential and residential structures with any claim to be part of the cultural heritage amounted to $250 billion. (That estimate requires that most of the value of religious buildings and non-governmental educational buildings be considered heritage value.)

No doubt, the estimating methods used for national wealth purposes may understate the value of structures *qua* heritage. This must be true to some extent, because the procedures for estimating depreciated replacement cost (the concept used in the national wealth estimates) tend to overstate the depreciation of very old buildings and to understate the replacement costs of structures built in a different era. Suppose that the actual value, taking heritage value into consideration, is twice my arbitrary estimate or $500

---

[5] The Association of Art Museum Directors regularly surveys all art museums of consequence and receives responses from about 85 per cent of them. In 1988, the respondents had $4.6 billion of insurance on an estimated 48 per cent of their collections (by value). Accounting for non-responses, art owned by other types of museums, the value of art purchased and donated in the following year (about $200 million), and probable over-statement of the percentage of value insured, results in an estimate that the value of art in museums was $12 billion at the end of 1989; I estimate, arbitrarily, that works outside museums had a value four times that in museums.

[6] 'Fixed reproducible tangible wealth' (that is, structures and equipment) is estimated by the Bureau of Economic Analysis of the US Department of Commerce, using the 'perpetual inventory' method – that is, cumulating annual new investment, subtracting 'normal' depreciation and other losses, and revaluing the net stock annually on the basis of general price indices.

billion.[7] Then capital consumption allowances at 1 per cent of the stock (double the depreciation rate for works of art, on the ground that buildings cannot be easily protected from ageing), or $5 billion, would have been less than 0·05 per cent of GDP, hardly a huge number.

But Italy is very different. The value of the stock of works of art, excluding buildings, must be at least 25 times that in the United States, and conceivably as much as 100 times as great. The value of heritage buildings probably is considerably more than 100 times that in the United States. But the GDP of Italy is roughly 15 per cent that of the US. If the proper multiplier for Italy versus the US is 100, then capital consumption allowances in Italy would amount, at an annual depreciation rate of 0·5 per cent, to nearly 35 per cent of GDP. Even if the multiplier is a low 25, capital consumption allowances at 0·5 per cent would be nearly 9 per cent of GDP. The reality could be significantly higher even than the 35 per cent figure. It is inconceivable that gross investment in heritage is more than a small fraction of the capital consumption. Thus, at least for Italy and some other countries, the issue is non-trivial: the net consumption of cultural capital is considerable, and the costs that would have to be borne in order to maintain the capital stock are far greater than the country could afford.

It seems clear that the appropriate level of current spending for maintaining heritage must be very high in numerous countries. If the costs are so high, relative to GDP, even in a country that is among the rich like Italy, they are appalling in poorer countries that are well-endowed culturally, like Russia, and in very poor countries that have even modest cultural endowments. Consequently, the international demand for heritage services that could be provided within those countries, were the finance available, will not be satisfied solely on the basis of local decision-making.

---

[7] The more lunatic among American architectural preservationists consider that *any* structure built before 1945 (and many structures built since then) is part of the heritage and may not be altered or destroyed, regardless of its provenance or appearance.

The Natural Environment Parallel[8]

It may help to think about the international demand for heritage services by paying some attention to the parallels with the international demand for the services of the natural environment, notably 'unspoiled' places of great beauty or ecological value. Here too there are option, existence and bequest values that are not likely to be fully realised by ordinary market transactions. Often the places in question are in poor countries or poor parts of countries that are not poor. Poor or not, there are often bitter controversies about the appropriate uses of the sites, which is also the case with regard to heritage sites. In both cases, the value of the services, heritage or environmental, can be degraded significantly by congestion. There may be not only market failure but 'non-market failure' as well, that is, dysfunctional actions by governmental entities that ignore the demand for preservation, such as short-term satisfaction of local transport demand at the expense of heritage and the environment and refusal to use prices where rationing of access is essential.

In important ways, there are strong parallels with environmental economics. The physical objects that are considered heritage comprise non-substitutable resources. If they are permitted to deteriorate and disappear, these resources are being exhausted, like many of the things that concern environmentalists.

As is the case with the natural environment, it is quite impossible to prevent *all* depletion of *all* non-substitutable resources. Species become extinct even in a state of nature; brain cells die and are not replaced as we age; the amount of fuel in our star decreases inexorably. Similarly, it is not possible to protect all historic buildings and art works in remote locations, or which are located in places with extraordinarily unfavourable atmospheric conditions. War, fire, flood and other disasters will take their toll. And, most important, we cannot predict what succeeding generations will consider worthy of heritage status and protection.

As with environmental protection policy, in heritage protection policy it is necessary to answer a number of crucial questions if policy is to begin to approach optimality. There is the question of just how non-substitutable the heritage object is, or rather the shape

---

[8] Much of this section is adapted from material in Dick Netzer, 'Principles and Policies for Optimizing the Use of Venice by Rationing Access', *Richerche Economiche*, Vol. 46, January-June 1992.

of the marginal value curve of heritage objects of a given type. This raises difficult valuation problems, which in environmental economics has led to the development of the contingent valuation approach. Also, there is the issue of reversibility. Scientists often disagree about the extent to which a specific type of environmental damage can be reversed; we know that some types can be from our experience in developed countries with the clean-up of polluted rivers in recent decades. As for the artistic heritage, art is the work of the mind. We know that many scientific and other ideas are lost and re-invented, or invented in many places independently. Why should this not be true also of artistic ideas?

It is not possible to avoid the issue of the discount rate for long periods into the future. Most of the opportunity costs can be measured readily, but some cannot, as we see today regarding the global-warming question; this is surely the case for cities whose centres are largely occupied with heritage uses, for it is difficult to estimate the benefits from alternative uses.

As in environmental policy, the *extent* of preservation in any specific case is often a policy choice, and affects the economic outcome substantially. Mossetto[9] notes the difference between the *re-use* that characterised earlier eras (for example, the use of the head of the statue of the Roman empress Livia as the face of an 11th-century Christ in a church in Germany), the *restoration* of some, but not all, deteriorated works common since then, and the more absolute *preservation* of all that is valuable in the heritage that is a more recent phenomenon. Mossetto establishes formally that the market in principle works adequately in the first two cases, but not in the third. Heritage policy, like environmental policy, tends today to be of the third case, which requires non-market intervention.

Congestion and the conflicts over use are widespread in both policy arenas. For decades, Venice has been the site of some of the most intense of such conflicts, with the heavy use of the lagoon for industrial purposes that are demonstrably destructive of heritage between 1945 and the very recent past, continued heavy use for mass recreation (rather like a theme park) and élite, heritage-based

---

[9] Gianfranco Mossetto, 'The Economic Dilemma of Heritage Preservation', in Alan Peacock and Ilde Rizzo (eds.), *Cultural Economics and Cultural Policies,* Dordrecht: Kluwer Academic Publishers, 1994.

cultural tourism, the last based to a considerable extent on international demand.

Conflicts over the Natural Environment: Sub-Saharan Africa and Antarctica

With regard to the natural environment, there frequently are similar conflicts between intensive and extensive tourist uses, and between tourist and non-tourist uses, such as wilderness areas in sub-Saharan Africa, where the conflict between tourist uses and subsistence agriculture, grazing and poaching, is typically severe and growing, given the extremely high rate of population increase in all of sub-Saharan Africa.

However, perhaps the most spectacular example of conflicts over use, in this case involving only international demand, is Antarctica. There are four conflicting uses of Antarctica, two long-standing, one potential and the fourth, tourism, quite recent and rapidly increasing. The first is the continent's rôle, together with its surrounding waters, in the Earth's climate and food chain. It is not clear how much conflict there is between this rôle and the other present uses – although some environmentalists believe that the conflict is real and serious – but the conflict between the potential use, for mining, and this rôle would surely be considered serious. The second use is as a vast science park, which has been important since the 1950s. There is, of course, no mining at present and the governing treaty prohibits any such exploitation.

In absolute numbers, tourism is small, certainly by the standards of a Venice – only a few thousand visitors each season. However, tourism has been increasing at a rapid rate, with the encouragement of the Chilean and Argentinian authorities, who authorise landings at their research bases on the Antarctic peninsula and are the countries from which the tourist ships sail. The scientific community believes that the present number of tourist visits already seriously threatens wildlife at some sites on the Antarctic peninsula, diverts the small number of scientific staff from their main duties, and substantially adds to the environmental loads created by the scientific uses of the continent. The scientists worry that, even if the environmental loadings imposed by the scientific personnel do not seriously conflict with the continent's rôle in planetary ecology, the marginal increment from tourism will make the conflict a serious one, and cause limits to be placed on the size of scientific staffs.

144

Like the case of Venice, there are conflicts between the pure public good – the climate and food chain rôle – and all the other uses, which do or can damage the public good, like overgrazing the commons. Like the Venice case, the mechanics of imposing stringent limits on the number of tourist visits to Antarctica are simple. But also like Venice, there are conflicting interests among those who are concerned with private goods, or mixed public and private goods – tour operators and Chileans and Argentinians seeking rents, tourists wishing to visit an 'unspoiled wilderness', scientists with a stake in research that is best done in Antarctica (the traditional industry of the continent), and entrepreneurs who would like to explore for minerals.[10]

In other wilderness areas, the conflict over uses and users is more like that in Venice, between the élite tourists – that is, those willing to pay a great deal in money, time and discomfort to enjoy the 'true wilderness' experience (like the residential tourists who stay in expensive Venice hotels long enough to experience Venice as a cultural good) – and the mass tourists, those content with a more fleeting and superficial exposure. As in Venice, very different people gain rents from the different uses. As in Venice, there are (actual or potential) non-tourist uses that conflict with the tourist uses. In few cases involving access to the natural environment has explicit price rationing ever been considered. But often, there is significant implicit price rationing, in the form of the necessarily high costs of access to the more remote locations that the élite tourists prefer. This reduces congestion, but does nothing to help finance the services that the international visitors demand.

Mechanisms to Realise International Demand

Market Approaches

The proposition that there are external benefits to transactions between heritage producers and consumers that will not be reflected in the prices paid in markets rests in part on the assumption that price discrimination is difficult or impossible, that all consumers

---

[10] Antarctic tourism could be ended abruptly by marginal-cost pricing of rescue services when accidents occur. The costs per incident (measured by the diversion of staff and fuel from scientific work) are many millions of dollars. Were the tour operators compelled to pay these costs, or insure against them, the price of a place on a tour might be 20 or 30 times as high as at present.

pay the same prices for the specified service. But this is frequently not an inevitable condition. If, for example, it is feasible to make foreign visitors pay substantially higher prices and those visitors place very high values on their own option, existence and bequest demand for the specified heritage services, at least some of those utilities can be internalised in market transactions. Private (and some public) providers of heritage services, or services ancillary to the heritage services themselves, are well aware of this, and have been for years. Hence, the large difference in *'vaporetti'* fares paid by residents and non-residents in Venice, the customary unavailability of concessionary admission charges to non-residents (other than students) in most countries, the far higher admission, hotel and other charges paid by Western visitors in some of the former communist countries (even in the market-oriented Czech Republic). If these additional revenues can be captured from service providers in the form of taxes and devoted to the financing of the heritage services, some part of this type of market failure is reduced or eliminated.

Radical Tax Innovations Required

That, however, may require some radical innovations in public finance systems. The 'modern' national tax system comprising harmonised income and value-added taxes, social security payroll taxes and high excise taxes on spirits, tobacco and petrol, almost all collected by central governments at uniform rates across the country (if not the continent), are very poorly suited to capture what really are 'location rents' generated in particular places by the demand from rich visitors. What is necessary, spectacularly so in Venice, is explicit local collection of large fractions of the economic rent of land – that is, land-value taxation. Instead there is no such taxation, and peppercorn rents for the appropriation of the public pavement by retail establishments throughout Italy and many other countries.

Also in the spirit of using markets to finance heritage services would be more reliance on congestion charges and other forms of marginal-cost pricing. Although price discrimination is indeed widespread in connection with the consumption of heritage services, economically efficient marginal-cost pricing is conspicuously absent, as is the equally efficient public collection of the economic rent of land. This is notably true in poor countries, perhaps because of the very old tradition that only the powerless need pay taxes.[11]

Reliance on markets can help in another way: keeping historic buildings in income-generating use can help to ensure their proper maintenance and to provide some of the finance needed to do so. This is an old story in Britain and the Loire valley in France, but not in all countries. Recently in Venice there have been strenuous efforts to pursue this strategy, and there are proposals to find income-generating uses for the hundreds of officially protected but privately owned country villas in the Veneto region.

Regulation

Protecting heritage by compelling private owners to bear substantial expenses with little compensation is popular with some Western governments. However, it is usually so objectionable to owners, who may be politically effective in expressing their opposition, that one would expect such 'hard regulation' not to be used in defence of the heritage elements that have an unusually large foreign, rather than domestic, demand. Instead, 'hard regulation' is most likely to succeed where there is powerful local demand for it.[12]

Throsby has noted a form of regulation described as 'soft regulation' – that is, international agreements and codes of behaviour that encourage national governments to do their best to protect the cultural heritage.[13] This, of course, is another form of the exhortation to behave well that international organisations and conferences fondly believe make a difference to outcomes. Perhaps it does make a difference in rich countries that are disposed to be good world citizens, like Canada, Australia and the Nordic countries. I am inclined to be sceptical of its effectiveness elsewhere, especially in poor countries. Surely, it will fall on deaf

---

[11] Some years ago while working in Pakistan, I discovered that neither custom duties nor internal excises were paid on equipment used in playing tennis, golf and polo, nor on gold and precious stones. But footballs and cooking oil were heavily taxed.

[12] For example, regulation to preserve the architecture of historic residential neighbourhoods may encourage gentrification and thus enrich the property owners subject to preservation orders. This regulation will be politically durable.

[13] David Throsby, 'Making It Happen: The Pros and Cons of Regulation in Urban Heritage Conservation', in J. M. Schuster and J. de Monchaux (eds.), *Tools for Preservation of the National Heritage*, Hanover, NH: University Press of New Great Britain, 1997.

ears in the numerous poor countries that have the form of government Peter Bauer called 'kleptocracies' – that is, government by thieves.

International Private Philanthropy

For many years, well-off nationals of rich countries and public charities of various types have spent substantial amounts to preserve important heritage elements in countries that are not their own. Venice has been a specially favoured beneficiary of private philanthropy, notably in the aftermath of floods and other emergencies. But there are many other heritage sites that have been favoured by individual and organised private philanthropy, in some cases in efforts persisting for years. The only issue of public policy is whether the giver's own country affords similar tax advantages to international philanthropy that it provides for charitable gifts for heritage elements located within that country. In the United States, where tax incentives for private philanthropy are very generous, there is in practice no distinction based on the location of the heritage that is the object of charity, so long as the funds pass through a US registered charity (which may be one organised for the sole purpose of assisting heritage preservation in other countries, such as the body called 'Save Venice') or go to a religious organisation, wherever that is located. In other countries, where the tax advantages of giving to domestic charity are less generous than in the US, there often is even more restrictive tax treatment of gifts destined for use abroad. For example, an American resident will enjoy tax advantages if he or she gives works of art to European museums, say, the Louvre; but generally Europeans do not enjoy tax reliefs which would benefit similar US institutions.

Intergovernmental Transfers

There is a strong case, in the theory of 'fiscal federalism', for grants from the government of one country to support heritage protection in another, to encourage the recipient country to generate unmarketable benefits of heritage protection that extend beyond national boundaries. In some cases, the transnational positive real externalities may exceed the benefits that can be appropriated within the country in question. This argues for systematic attention to schemes for transfers. By 'systematic' I mean arrangements that are more continuous than appeals for emergency assistance when disasters strike, like floods in Venice, or the likely world-wide appeal for funds for the restoration of Angkor Wat soon after peace comes to Cambodia.

The theory of fiscal federalism is a set of concepts dear to the hearts of American public finance economists, and no doubt sounds hopelessly parochial.[14] As a tool of scientific inquiry, fiscal federalism moves public economics from the study of a public sector with no institutional content to the study of one that resembles the real world. All Western states operate with some degree of fiscal federalism – that is, independent decision-making by sub-national public authorities on the provision or financing of some types of public services.[15] There are wide differences among countries in the extent of formal decentralisation of decision-making and perhaps even wider differences in the extent to which fiscal outcomes – the results of the decision-making processes – differ within countries. But there is fiscal federalism everywhere, and it applies to the rôle of the public sector in the provision and financing of heritage protection and artistic production. There is no Western country in which the central government has no rôle, and no Western country in which the central government is the *only* public sector organisation concerned with heritage and the arts.

In part, this is because public expenditure for these purposes is so small, relative to either gross domestic product or to total public expenditure, that even poorly financed local authorities can play a part. But, in addition, it reflects an unspoken awareness on the part of voters and politicians that there are advantages in a régime of fiscal federalism for culture. As with many other public policies and institutions, there is implicit recognition of some economic truths. The essential economic truth is that efficiency in resource allocation requires some degree of fiscal federalism.

The micro-economic framework is that of individualistic welfare economics. That framework allows for government action to redistribute income in money or in kind, action that may reflect efficiency in choice by households, but which may have nothing to

---

[14] Much of the following discussion is adapted from Dick Netzer, 'Local, Central and Supra-National Governments in Heritage Protection and Artistic Production', paper presented at a Workshop on the Economics of the Arts and Culture, CISEP, Instituto Superior de Economia e Gestao, Universidade Tecnica de Lisboa, November 1994.

[15] I refer here to true states, not to mini-states.

do with efficiency at all. Otherwise, government action is appropriate only if there are no markets (the pure public goods case) or if there is serious market failure. In this paradigm, the purpose of government intervention on efficiency grounds is to provide the goods and services that would be provided in perfectly functioning markets – that is, what consumers want and will pay for. Efficiency is achieved when the various conditions for equality at the margin are satisfied. Most of us recognise that a reasonable goal, in most circumstances, is the second best, which of course is true of many other markets as well.

The Tax-Price

Designers of policies for government intervention need to ensure that the unmarketable utilities the cultural sector produces are forthcoming by helping consumers in their capacities as voters to confront the 'right' prices in making decisions through the public sector (the so-called 'tax-price'). That is, in a referendum, if the unmarketable utilities are estimated to be worth £20 per year to the median voter, voters should not be asked to approve subsidies that will cost £100, or £5.

An important determinant of the correct tax-price is the geographic reach of the benefits from a particular type of public expenditure, as perceived by consumers-as-voters. Most types of public expenditure, cultural as well as other, do not provide benefits that are uniform throughout an entire nation-state, but have a degree of geographic specificity. The unmarketable values associated with heritage are likely to be affected by how close one's residence is to the heritage element. Some benefits are narrowly confined spatially, while some are realised over a wide area; the proportions differ for different types of cultural goods and services and different subsidies. The obviously efficient solution is to finance the benefits that are narrowly confined spatially from local authority taxes and the benefits that are realised over a wide area from taxes collected over that wide area, that is, by regional or national (or even supra-national) governments. At each level of government, the expenditure decision should be made on the assumption that each level will be financing the appropriate proportion of the total expenditure for the activity: that is, voters at that level will be asked to finance only the benefits they receive in their capacities as taxpayers to that level of government. The tax-price at that point will be the right one.

In the real world of fiscal federalism, highly imperfect mechanisms are the rule and tax-prices are seldom optimal. However, the real-world results do not destroy the case for an efficient scheme of fiscal federalism as the proper way to deal with market failure in regard to heritage.

The concept of fiscal federalism is as appropriate to the rôle of supra-national government, in its relation to national governments and to sub-national governments within nation-states, as it is to the relation between the central government of a nation-state and its political divisions. Experience has shown that there are public goods that can be better provided by supra-national institutions than by national ones, like the matters that occupy the International Court of Justice, some aspects of international and national security, and important aspects of international economic relations.

There are also issues connected not with actual production of the public goods by supra-national organisations, but with the funding of more output of certain public goods (and less of certain public bads) than individual nation-states will fund by themselves. Most often this is done by donor countries making grants directly to recipient countries, but sometimes it is done through supra-national institutions. A spectacular current case is the international effort by the West to persuade some former (or still) Communist countries to close down or replace dangerous nuclear plants, by offering them money and other help.

A Case for Supra-National Intervention?

For most cultural goods and services, it is hard to see much of a case for supra-national intervention. There are perhaps some desperately poor countries in the Third World which simply cannot afford the costs of reasonable-quality arts festivals or permanent performing companies for which there is some real local demand. However, that situation does not apply to the so-called 'middle-income' developing countries in Asia, North Africa and Latin America, nor to any country in Europe, including the former Communist countries: the cost of the needed subsidies (if any) for such activities is likely to be very low relative to total public expenditure in that country. Moreover, the benefits from the activities that spill over national boundaries are likely to be small or non-existent, making it

151

difficult to justify external subsidy on anything like efficiency grounds.[16]

A major exception to this concerns heritage protection and preservation of the artistic heritage, as noted throughout this paper: people in rich countries do have an interest in heritage protection. This is not an equity issue. If poor people/places give a very low priority to heritage protection, it is not consistent with the ethics of the equity concept for national or supra-national governments to give them a lot of heritage protection and not much of the public goods they really do value highly. But it *is* consistent with efficiency to do so by providing matching grants that dramatically reduce the price of heritage protection to the recipient units of government, thus exploiting the high price-elasticity of demand implied by 'a very low priority' for heritage protection.

From an institutional and operational standpoint, it inevitably is difficult to organise supra-national intervention in the cultural sphere in general, and not much less difficult with regard to heritage preservation, except in catastrophes when all the normal rules and constraints tend to be ignored, at least in the immediate aftermath of the catastrophe. Even so, the conceptual apparatus of fiscal federalism seems appropriate.

The price-elasticity of demand for heritage preservation is likely to be quite high in poor countries, so supra-national grants that lower the tax-price within the poor country could leverage a great deal more local spending, and political and administrative co-operation. Moreover, because the marginal utility of heritage preservation is low in a country that has a great deal of heritage to preserve, a low tax-price at the margin is needed to make that country willing to spend more. If a country is a poor one with a great deal of heritage to preserve, the tax-price may have to be very low indeed for the country to act as those in other countries would prefer. But grants that lower the tax-price to zero are not likely to produce sensible results, nor are grants that amount to 'lump-sum transfers' (which do not require the recipient governments to change their behaviour in specified ways).

---

[16] Indeed, the welfare of people in the rich countries is likely to be increased, as has happened in the past, if talented artists in countries that are poor (either temporarily or permanently) emigrate to the rich countries and pursue their artistic careers there.

Supra-national action in the cultural field is quite vulnerable to rent-seeking behaviour, like supra-national action in other areas (such as environmental issues) in which the rent-seekers can persuade themselves and others that their behaviour is in the service of a noble cause (and unlike famine relief workers, the cultural activists do not expose themselves to danger or even much discomfort). In practice, much of the supra-national funding, in Europe especially, has been devoted to 'cultural planning' and other bureaucratic activities, with outputs of public goods that must be close to zero.

A Case in Point: Russia

The immediate cases in point are Russia and, to varying degrees, other former Communist countries. In most of them, there are large numbers of historic buildings that have been extremely poorly maintained (or deliberately harmed) throughout the years of Communist rule – in Russia, even before that, given the incompetence of the Czarist régime. In Russia itself, there are large numbers of works of art in structures that have been so badly maintained that the art works must have suffered considerably, and there are large numbers of privately owned art works that have been exposed to damage over many years. Although the export of privately owned works of art was prohibited in the Soviet Union from its earliest days, and although the sale of art works within the country, except by the artists who made the work, was very restricted, there apparently was no law against *owning* works of art. Large numbers of such works, created both before and after 1917, remain in private ownership.

Since there was almost no conservation work done except in a very few museums, and that only on a limited basis, whatever damage that there was remained unrepaired. Clearly, without substantial assistance from other countries, conservation and preservation will not have a high priority in the troubled economic conditions in Russia. Indeed, the rate of loss may accelerate, at least to the extent that works of art are not exported.

In the light of budgetary retrenchment and reductions in support by rich countries of the cultural sector within their own borders, it would seem unlikely that transfers in support of the cultural endowments of other countries will be favourably received. Nonetheless, a strong case can be made that the externalities are

153

important to the present and future populations of the countries that would be net donors.

There is an analogy, in respect of possible assistance to Russia for preservation of the cultural heritage, with the programme of US aid to Russia for dismantling nuclear weapons and safe disposal of nuclear material. In that programme, the benefits to the US and the rest of the world are clear, and the assistance has the considerable advantages of providing important work for highly trained people who are otherwise likely to suffer heavily in the economic dislocations in Russia (and who have the potential for contributing to political instability). Moreover, their experience in nuclear dismantling and disposal will be a form of human capital, the future output of which has potential export markets.

This is also true, although less dramatically, of foreign aid for cultural preservation. The work will employ, in some cases with some retraining, skilled people, who also are likely to suffer considerably in Russia's economic difficulties, namely visual artists, art historians, curators and some of the most skilled construction workers. Here too there can be the development of expertise that can be used in other countries, and generate export earnings.[17]

This suggests that there are benefits to the countries with massive, but endangered, cultural endowments in increasing their own efforts in support of their cultural endowments, even aside from the obvious benefits connected with tourism. The economic benefits from increased numbers of tourist visits may be negative in congested Venice, but the benefits remain positive in many places where congestion is moderate or non-existent. The greater those benefits and the less impoverished the country, the more leverage modest financial assistance from other countries, or supra-national entities, will have. But do not take anything in this paper as an argument for still more international meetings of bureaucrats.

---

[17] No doubt some of the human capital would be lost to Russia from emigration. There is a parallel in one American experience. There was a long period in which virtually all skilled stone masons in New York and some other American cities were recent immigrants from Italy, which seemed to be the only country in which those skills were fostered. This was encouraged by the immigration laws, which gave a marked advantage to people with skills in short supply in the US who had job offers from American employers. In the last 10 years, changes in the immigration laws encouraged American firms that do stone restoration work (usually headed by people who themselves were immigrants from Italy) to train others for that work.

The Poverty of 'Development Economics'

'a major contribution to the literature on the problems facing Third World countries'.
The Economic Journal

Deepak Lal

1. From the end of the Second World War to the early 1970s, most Third World countries adopted 'inward looking' policies. These policies then began to break down until collapse of the Second World in the late 1980s started a '...breathtaking worldwide movement from the plan to the market'.

2. The new liberal international economic order is similar to that in the nineteenth century in that free movement of goods and capital prevails. But immigration controls inhibit the movement of labour.

3. In the last twenty years, the performance of developing countries as a whole relative to OECD countries has much improved, largely because of big improvements in East Asia and South Asia. The 1980s were a 'lost decade' for sub Saharan Africa and Latin America though prospects are now better in both areas.

4. Liberalising Third World countries can now attract private portfolio and direct investment. Except for Africa, private flows of foreign capital are more important than official 'aid'.

5. The final 'nail in the coffin' of the 'old' development economics was realisation of the immense corruption it breeds. Dirigisme necessarily results in politicisation and rent-seeking.

6. The 'consensual policy package' of the 1990s stresses state provision of essential 'public goods'; otherwise, economic activity should be left to private agents.

7. Past dirigisme led to disorder, eroding the state's fiscal base. The resulting crises were often the occasions for liberalisation. A 'big bang' approach to liberalisation may be necessary: otherwise the state may cease liberalising once the immediate crisis is past.

8. 'Adjustment with a human face' is the new slogan of those who want to create Western style welfare states in the Second and Third Worlds at a time when First World countries, where the welfare system has been captured by the middle classes, are embarking on reform.

9. Many East Asian countries have shown that mass poverty can be eradicated within a generation. 'A market-based liberal economic order...can cure the age-long problem of structural mass poverty.'

10. Western democracy embodies tensions between the notions of the state as a civil association and as an enterprise association. The '...mere transfer of Western forms of governance and their attendant ideology is as unlikely to secure the market in the Third World as it is in the First.'

The Institute of Economic Affairs

2 Lord North Street, Westminster, London SW1P 3LB
Telephone: 0171 799 3745 Facsimile: 0171 799 2137
E-mail: iea@iea.org.uk Internet: http://www.iea.org.uk   ISBN 0-255 36410-5

£12.00

Democratic Values and the Currency

Michael Portillo

with a Postscript by

Martin Feldstein

1. The single currency is not 'merely an economic device' but '...a project in re-shaping the way our Continent is governed'.
2. The 'federalism' now being pursued at European level is 'highly centralising and owes much to the Monnet-functionalist approach'.
3. Much of the momentum behind European integration derives from the fear of war. But Europe is more secure from inter-continental conflict than ever before because it is composed of democracies and '...it is inconceivable that democracies would go to war with one another'.
4. European integration is '...not the means to achieve the security of our Continent'. Because the form of integration reduces democratic control, rather than abolishing nationalism it risks stirring it up.
5. For democracy to work, people have to have more than just a vote. Resentment and unrest will be the result if policies are made by bodies '...thought to be too distant, or made by people who are not democratically accountable at all'.
6. Motivation for the single currency is political, not economic. It is '...a bigger step towards centralised decision-making than any that has been taken before'.
7. Monetary policy will become the responsibility of a European Union central bank. Constraints on borrowing will restrict member-countries' freedom to decide either tax rates or spending levels. Because there is no single labour market, and the flexibility of currency adjustment will have been lost, the '...full impact of recession will ...fall on unemployment'.
8. Electors will feel 'resentful and cheated' when they cannot through their votes influence economic policy or change the policy-makers.
9. Trying to establish democratic accountability at European level is not the answer. 'Europe' does not constitute a nation. 'No parliament spanning from Dublin to Athens ...is capable of satisfying the democratic requirements and aspirations of each of our populations'.
10. Though the EU is composed of democracies, the Union itself is undemocratic. Transferring decisions from member-states to the Union reduces democratic accountability with the danger of providing '...a breeding ground for nationalism and extremism'.

The Institute of Economic Affairs

2 Lord North Street, Westminster, London SW1P 3LB
Telephone: 0171 799 3745 Facsimile: 0171 799 2137
E-mail: iea@iea.org.uk Internet: http://www.iea.org.uk

ISBN 0-255 36412-1

£4.00

The Conservative Government's Economic Record: An End of Term Report

Nicholas Crafts

1. The first half of the eighteen years of Conservative government saw a radical departure from the economic policies of all earlier postwar governments with a new emphasis on the supply side. In the later years, the '...Thatcher experiment' was 'refined and extended'.

2. From the 1950s to the 1970s there were 'mistaken economic policies and institutional deficiencies' which had to be corrected if Britain's relative economic decline was to end.

3. In those early years, physical capital was subsidised, state ownership was widespread, 'national champions' and prestige research projects were promoted. Governments failed to reform industrial relations or taxation.

4. Vocational training was poor, labour was used inefficiently, and industrial relations arrangements increased unemployment despite government efforts to '...suppress the problem through incomes policies'.

5. The Conservatives strengthened '...incentives and market disciplines' and reduced subsidies in actions which have '...some support from modern growth economics'. They failed, however, to introduce competition in some privatised industries and (in the 1990s) to reduce the burden of taxation on growth.

6. Employment policy focussed on reducing equilibrium unemployment, abandoning incomes policies. Less commendable were efforts to 'hide unemployment'.

7. Counter-inflationary efforts were '...much less well-conceived than either labour market or supply-side policy'. The government failed to choose suitable policy targets and was reluctant to surrender political control of monetary and exchange rate policies.

8. A striking feature was a marked upturn in labour productivity growth in manufacturing which reduced the productivity gap between Britain and other countries. But there was no comparable upturn in service sector productivity growth.

9. Changes in the '...bargaining environment and associated developments in industrial relations' seem to have had a major effect on manufacturing productivity. Product market deregulation was also important.

10. The Conservative years have '...left long term growth prospects in Britain better than would have seemed possible eighteen years ago.' 'Microeconomic radicalism paid off handsomely' though macroeconomic management was less successful.

The Institute of Economic Affairs

2 Lord North Street, Westminster, London SW1P 3LB
Telephone: 0171 799 3745 Facsimile: 0171 799 2137
E-mail: iea@iea.org.uk Internet: http://www.iea.org.uk

ISBN 0-255 36413-X

£4.00